THE BOUNTIFUL KITCHEN

TO MY MOOMIN MAMA, FOR EVERYTHING.

FIRST PUBLISHED IN GREAT BRITAIN IN 2016
BY KYLE BOOKS
AN IMPRINT OF KYLE CATHIE LIMITED
192-198 VAUXHALL BRIDGE ROAD
LONDON SW1V 1DX
GENERAL.ENQUIRIES@KYLEBOOKS.COM
WWW.KYLEBOOKS.CO.UK

10 9 8 7 6 5 4 3 2 1

ISBN: 978 0 85783 359 4

A CIP CATALOGUE RECORD FOR THIS TITLE IS
AVAILABLE FROM THE BRITISH LIBRARY

TEXT © LIZZIE KAMENETZKY 2016
PHOTOGRAPHS © LAURA EDWARDS 2016
DESIGN © KYLE BOOKS 2016

EDITOR **VICKY ORCHARD**
DESIGN **HELEN BRATBY**
PHOTOGRAPHY **LAURA EDWARDS**
FOOD STYLING **LIZZIE KAMENETZKY**
PROPS STYLING **POLLY WEBB-WILSON**
PRODUCTION **GEMMA JOHN AND NIC JONES**

COLOUR REPRODUCTION BY ALTA LONDON
PRINTED AND BOUND IN CHINA BY
1010 INTERNATIONAL PRINTING LTD

THE BOUNTIFUL KITCHEN

DELICIOUS IDEAS TO TURN ONE DISH INTO TWO

LIZZIE KAMENETZKY

PHOTOGRAPHY BY LAURA EDWARDS

KYLE BOOKS

CONTENTS

INTRODUCTION

'The most remarkable thing about my mother is that for thirty years she served the family nothing but leftovers. The original meal has never been found.'

Calvin Trillin,
American food writer and humorist

I absolutely adore leftovers. There, I've said it. A fridge full of bits and bobs, of small bowls of saved deliciousness just waiting to be turned into something wonderful. Almost all of the hard work has already been done and now you can reap the rewards. I think that fridge-raid cooking produces some of my most creative and wonderful dishes, most of them almost entirely by a mix of happy accident and necessity.

As testimony to how even an empty fridge can bear fruit, the other day when proofreading this book, I was starving and had pretty much nothing in my fridge save for a tub of mayonnaise and a gem lettuce. Not to be thwarted, I hunted in the cupboard and found some basmati rice and a tin of tuna fish. One of the strangest but most delicious lunches I have had in a while – warm rice tossed with a splodge of mayo, flaked olive-oily tuna and finely shredded lettuce.

The sad thing is that, as a word, 'leftovers' sound so humble, as to even be dowdy and unloved. If we are honest, it tends not to be a word to excite passion and get the heart racing. It speaks of dishes made out of desperation, of can't-quite-be-bothered-ness and of reheating tired ingredients from the day before. I wish desperately there was another word, something that could convey the true magic and joy of cooking with leftovers. Once you realise the full potential, the freedom and fun you can have with a little left over from a wonderful meal, the way that you cook will be revolutionised.

I think my love of leftovers is twofold. Firstly I am a really generous cook – I tend to make a little extra of everything, just in case. Both because I can't bear the thought of anyone being hungry, but much more selfishly because I want the wonderful leftovers that a generously cooked supper can bring. That, and the fact that I have never accurately managed the art of cooking the right quantity of rice for four people, means that I always have leftovers in my fridge to play with.

The way we shop has a lot to do with why so many people are not embracing the leftovers way. For me, the idea of a weekly shop, of planned menus and meals, is one of tyranny and waste. And here is the second reason why I am a leftovers addict: I loathe wasted food. I have always found that shopping to cook a different meal for every night of the week runs the risk that not only do ingredients you have bought sit in your fridge unused until they perish, but also that when you have leftovers from supper they more likely than not end up being thrown away, ironically because you have something different planned for the next day that you don't want to waste.

It wasn't until we started to photograph this book that I understood just how my natural way of cooking drastically reduces food waste. Normally at the end of a day's shoot, I set up a little 'shop' from which all the team can help themselves. All the ingredients that didn't get used, the half open bags of this and that, and, of course, the finished dishes that didn't get eaten, to be taken home as leftovers. But at the end of a day shooting the recipes for this book, there was almost nothing left, much to the chagrin of the girls and boys! Every master recipe that we cooked was half devoured before the remainder was forcibly removed away from fork distance to be turned into the next recipe on the shot list, which was in turn devoured. No waste. One recipe really was becoming two or even three!

This way of cooking is ultimately extremely thrifty, flexible and good for the bank balance, the planet and your confidence and skills as a ready-for-anything cook. Yes, it might seem daunting at first to release yourself from the shackles of a meal plan, even crazy perhaps. We are all busy – work, family, children, social activities – and it might seem scary not to have fully planned what you are going to cook. But trust me, once you start breaking away from the bonds of over-shopping and pre-planning you will feel such a sense of relief and happiness that you will never go back.

Of course you still need to plan a little bit. As much as I love the idea of Mrs Trillin's eternal leftovers, the reality is that in order to have leftovers you need to cook. So for three or four nights of the week, plan to cook something delicious and then for the rest of the week experiment with the wonderful leftovers and fridge raiding!

The key to those days when you open your fridge to investigate what you might have to turn into something tasty for supper does rely on one thing. The store cupboard. People bang on about store cupboard suppers, and then they ask you to have all manner of weird and wonderful ingredients that, in reality, you may never have unless you either love them or buy them specially.

That said, a well-stocked cupboard will change your life. You don't have to go mad, just staples. Things that, when added to leftovers you already have, can create something new and different. Basic spices, tins of chickpeas and beans, rice, pasta, tins of tomatoes and a few sauces or mustards are the sort of things I mean.

I also try and use my fridge as a sort of store cupboard – stocking it with a few key things I know are great on a fridge raid, but things that will keep for a good length of time if you don't use them straight away, such as bacon or chorizo, yogurt, cream cheese, Parmesan and few simple vegetables or bags of salad that are easy to eat up. That and a few pots of living herbs and you are away!

The other really, really important thing to remember is not to be tied to a recipe. That might sound weird as after all, writing recipes is what I do. Yes, a recipe should absolutely work and be delicious if you follow it to the letter, but that does not mean that it won't be equally delicious if you go off-piste a bit.

Savoury recipes in particular are forgiving and ultimately flexible, meaning you can tailor them to suit all tastes as well as to what you might happen to have in the fridge or cupboard. You will notice that in all my recipes, but especially in the leftover ones, there are lots of different ideas and alternatives. This is about getting creative, using what you have, swapping and trying different flavours. Cream can almost always be crème fraîche, yogurt or soured cream. Greens can be any leafy or green veg, swap rice for pasta or chickpeas for beans. Really and truly, almost anything goes.

Thinking seasonally helps too. When something is in season and at its best, such as asparagus, tomatoes, peas and beans, Jersey Royals, Brussels sprouts or purple sprouting broccoli, buy them, in small quantities, and use them in your fridge raids.

I hope you will love this book as much as I enjoyed writing it and will also enjoy playing around with the recipes and creating your own leftover favourites. I have never really analysed the way I cook, but the more I wrote, the more I realised that this really is a better way to cook.

STORE + FRIDGE

This is not an exhaustive list of all the useful things you can have in your cupboard and fridge to help change the way you cook, but it is a good place to start.

SIMPLE SPICES
Cumin seeds, coriander seeds, chilli flakes, star anise, fennel seeds, cinnamon sticks, turmeric, paprika, cardamom pods

TINS
Tomatoes, chickpeas, beans, lentils, coconut milk, tuna

PACKET AND BOX
Eggs, basmati rice, risotto rice, pasta, noodles, grains

FLAVOUR BOOSTERS
Tomato purée, mustards, anchovies, olives, horseradish, harissa, capers, cornichons, stock cubes

BOTTLES
Olive oil, vinegars, soy sauce, Worcestershire sauce, ketchup, mayonnaise, Tabasco sauce

BAKING
Flours, caster sugar, brown sugar, vanilla extract, raisins or sultanas/dried fruit, ground almonds and other nuts, oats, stem ginger, maple syrup, golden syrup, yeast, chocolate

IN THE DARK
Onions, shallots, garlic, potatoes/parsnips/celeriac, fresh tomatoes

ON THE SILL
Lemon/lime/orange, pots of growing herbs – basil, thyme, parsley, tarragon, rosemary, chives

CHILLED
Butter, milk, cream/cream cheese/yogurt/crème fraîche, bacon/pancetta/chorizo, hot-smoked salmon or mackerel, cheese such as Parmesan/Gruyère/blue cheese/feta/Cheddar/goat's, greens such as cabbage/broccoli/sprouts/kale, courgette/aubergine, salad and leaves, ginger and chillies

DEEP FREEZE
Peas, beans, puff pastry, ice cream, frozen berries, fresh breadcrumbs, frozen prawns

GRIDDLED CHICKEN WITH KALE, TARRAGON + HAZELNUT PESTO
LINGUINE WITH KALE PESTO + CRISPY CHICKEN SKIN
CHICKEN + WHITE BEANS

ROAST CHICKEN WITH LEMON + TARRAGON
ROAST CHICKEN + MUSHROOM RISOTTO
QUICK CHICKEN, PURPLE SPROUTING BROCCOLI + STICKY CHILLI STIR-FRY

LAMB KOFTES WITH MINT + YOGURT
SPICED LAMB + HUMMUS WRAPS
SORT OF MOUSSAKA

CHARGRILLED LAMB SHOULDER
LAMB KARAHI
FATTEH

SALT-CRUSTED LAMB RACKS WITH SALSA VERDE
WARM LAMB + WATERCRESS SALAD
QUICK LAMB PIZZAIOLA

SPICE-CRUSTED RUMP CAP WITH PUY LENTIL SALAD
TAGLIATA
BEEF WITH BÉARNAISE SAUCE + CHIPS

SLOW-COOKED BEEF RAGÙ
BEEF + BARLEY SOUP
SMOKY BEEF EMPANADAS

STICKY BRAISED SHORT RIBS
THAI BEEF SALAD
BEEF SUMMER ROLLS

SLOW-ROAST JUNIPER + FENNEL SEED PORK BELLY
GOULASH
SHREDDED PORK + APPLE BUNS

PAN-RAOSTED PORK CHOPS WITH APPLES + ONIONS
SPICED PORK WITH HARISSA CHICKPEAS
RAINBOW SALAD

LEMONGRASS + GINGER PORK
SZECHUAN PORK + AUBERGINE BITES
PORK + PRAWN STEAMED DUMPLINGS

CHICKEN HAINAN
SOUL SOUP
COCONUT + CHILLI CHICKEN POTS

LAND

Pesto is so much more than the classic basil and pine nut variety. I love experimenting with different green veg and hard cheeses to see what new deliciousness awaits. You don't have to use all kale – swap some for parsley instead, or try using Brussels sprouts! You can also use Pecorino or Manchego as an alternative to Parmesan.

GRIDDLED CHICKEN WITH KALE, TARRAGON + HAZELNUT PESTO

SERVES **4**, PLUS LEFTOVERS
15 MINUTES TO MAKE
25 MINUTES TO COOK

4 FREE-RANGE SKIN ON CHICKEN
   BREASTS
SEA SALT AND FRESHLY GROUND BLACK
   PEPPER
500G NEW POTATOES
2 TABLESPOONS OLIVE OIL

FOR THE PESTO
200G CURLY KALE, CAVALO NERO OR
   BRUSSELS SPROUTS
2-3 SPRIGS OF TARRAGON, LEAVES
   STRIPPED
150-200ML EXTRA VIRGIN OLIVE OIL
2 GARLIC CLOVES, CRUSHED
70G HAZELNUTS, BLANCHED
100G PARMESAN CHEESE, GRATED
LEMON JUICE, TO TASTE

1. Remove the skin from the chicken breasts and keep for Linguine with Kale Pesto + Crispy Chicken Skin (page 14). Put the chicken breasts between pieces of clingfilm or baking parchment and bash with a rolling pin until about 1cm thick.

2. Tip the potatoes into a pan of cold salted water, bring to the boil and simmer until tender. Drain and crush with a fork and toss with most of the olive oil and some seasoning.

3. Heat a griddle pan over a high heat. Brush the chicken with the remaining oil, season well and griddle for 2-3 minutes on each side until just cooked. Set aside to rest.

4. Shred the kale and plunge into a pan of boiling water for a minute to just start to cook it, drain and refresh under cold water then whizz with the remaining ingredients. Season to taste with salt, pepper and lemon juice. Slice the chicken (hold back one breast for another time) and serve with the crushed potatoes and half of the pesto. Keep the remaining pesto for another recipe – it will keep in the fridge for up to a week.

tips Buy skin-on chicken breasts and remove the skin to use in leftovers recipes to add a hit of chicken flavour.

Slicing a chicken breast makes it go much further – 3 breasts will feed 4 people as a main meal but if you buy and cook 4 chicken breasts you can save one or even 1½ to use in leftover dishes.

ENOUGH LEFT OVER FOR:

LINGUINE WITH KALE PESTO + CRISPY CHICKEN SKIN
   (PAGE 14)
CHICKEN + WHITE BEANS (PAGE 16) »——→

It can be hard to find chicken breasts with the skin on these days, as if we are all afraid of them, when in reality they are one of the tastiest bits of the bird. By saving the skins from the meal on page 13, you can get all that savoury chicken-y hit into your pasta without the need to add any meat at all!

LINGUINE WITH KALE PESTO + CRISPY CHICKEN SKIN

SERVES 4
5 MINUTES TO MAKE
15 MINUTES TO COOK

SKIN FROM 4 FREE-RANGE CHICKEN
    BREASTS (PAGE 13)
350G LINGUINE OR OTHER PASTA
150-200G KALE + HAZELNUT PESTO
    (PAGE 13)
GRATED PARMESAN CHEESE, TO SERVE

1. Preheat the oven to 200°C/fan 180°C/gas 6. Put the chicken skin on a lipped baking sheet and put another baking sheet on top. Cook for 10–12 minutes until the skin is crispy. Pour off the fat into a small bowl and set the skin aside.

2. Cook the pasta in a saucepan of boiling salted water for 10–12 minutes until just cooked. Drain and toss with 1 tablespoon of the chicken fat, 1 tablespoon of cooking water and the pesto. Crush the chicken skin into crunchy pieces.

3. Divide the pasta between warmed bowls and scatter with the crispy skin and grated Parmesan.

tip If you haven't already made the pesto, make half the quantity in the recipe for Griddled Chicken with Kale, Tarragon + Hazelnut Pesto on page 13.

There is something so comforting about soft and creamy beans melting into sauces and stews. Canned beans are an absolute staple in my store cupboard and they are ideal for making leftovers suppers a doddle.

SERVES **4**
10 MINUTES TO MAKE
15 MINUTES TO COOK

CHICKEN + WHITE BEANS

1 TABLESPOON OLIVE OIL

100G CHORIZO, STREAKY BACON,
  PANCETTA OR SALAMI, FINELY
  CHOPPED

1 LARGE ONION, FINELY SLICED

2 GARLIC CLOVES, CRUSHED

A FEW SPRIGS OF THYME, PLUS EXTRA
  TO GARNISH

400G CAN OF WHITE BEANS (BUTTER
  OR CANNELLINI ARE PERFECT),
  DRAINED AND RINSED

200ML CHICKEN STOCK (PAGE 19)

1-1½ LEFTOVER GRIDDLED CHICKEN
  BREASTS (PAGE 13), FINELY SLICED

SPLASH OF DOUBLE CREAM OR A
  DOLLOP OF CRÈME FRAÎCHE

JUICE OF ½ LEMON

SEA SALT AND FRESHLY GROUND BLACK
  PEPPER

1. Heat the oil in a pan and fry the chorizo or other meaty bits for a few minutes until crispy. Remove with a slotted spoon and set aside. Add the onion to the pan and fry for 5 minutes until softened then add the garlic, thyme and the bacon and stir for 30 seconds.

2. Add the beans and stock and bubble for 5 minutes then add the sliced chicken, cream or crème fraîche and lemon juice. Season to taste and serve with the extra parsley scattered over the top.

tip If you haven't cooked the Griddled Chicken with Kale, Tarragon + Hazelnut Pesto on page 13 use 1 (or 2 small) free-range chicken breasts. Slice them thinly and pan-fry them with the onion at the start of the recipe.

A roast chicken is a universal joy. The transformation from humble bird to gloriously golden feast is wonderful to watch. Buy the best free-range chicken available as you can easily make three meals from the one purchase, so the cost is spread out and the flavour of the resulting roast is incomparable.

ROAST CHICKEN WITH LEMON + TARRAGON

SERVES **4**, PLUS LEFTOVERS
15 MINUTES TO MAKE
1 HOUR **25** MINUTES TO COOK

1 FREE-RANGE CHICKEN,
   WEIGHING ABOUT 2KG
2 TABLESPOONS UNSALTED BUTTER,
   SOFTENED
1 GARLIC CLOVE, CRUSHED
ZEST OF 2 LEMONS, PLUS JUICE OF 1
1 SMALL BUNCH OF TARRAGON
SEA SALT AND FRESHLY GROUND BLACK
   PEPPER
750G NUTTY NEW POTATOES (ANAYA OR
   PINK FIR APPLES ARE MY FAVOURITES)
150ML DRY WHITE WINE
400ML FRESH CHICKEN STOCK (SEE TIP)

tip To make chicken stock with the carcass, just break the bones into pieces and put in a deep pan with a chopped onion, carrot and celery (if you have them) and add any herbs, such as bay leaf, parsley stalks, sprigs of thyme or rosemary. Cover with water and simmer for 2 hours, skimming every so often. Strain and cool. Keep in the fridge for up to a week or freeze in small quantities.

1. Preheat the oven to 200°C/fan 180°C/gas 6. Take your chicken and use your fingers to separate the skin from the breast meat, working up under the skin from the neck end of the bird being careful not to tear the skin.

2. Mix the butter with the garlic and lemon zest. Finely chop two thirds of the tarragon and squidge that into the butter with plenty of sea salt and black pepper. Use your hands to push the butter up under the skin and smear it over the breast.

3. Put the chicken into a roasting tin, squeeze over the lemon juice then pop the lemon halves into the cavity. Scatter the new potatoes around the outside and pour over the wine and 100ml of the stock.

4. Roast for at least 1 hour or until the chicken is golden and just cooked – when you pierce the thickest part of the bird (between the thigh and breast) with a sharp knife the juices should run clear. Place onto a warmed platter and use a slotted spoon to put the potatoes around the outside. Leave to rest for at least 15 minutes, covered loosely in foil.

5. Put the tin with the cooking juices over a high heat and add the remaining stock and tarragon and bubble for a few minutes, adding any juices from the resting chicken.

6. When you have served the chicken, strip the carcass of all its remaining meat with your fingers and save any juices or gravy for leftover dishes.

ENOUGH LEFT OVER FOR:
ROAST CHICKEN + MUSHROOM RISOTTO (PAGE 20)
QUICK CHICKEN, PURPLE SPROUTING BROCCOLI +
   STICKY CHILLI STIR-FRY (PAGE 22) »——→

If rice is my go-to staple ingredient, then risotto has to be my favourite rice dish. A good risotto should be creamy and soft, never sticky or heavy. This is the BEST mushroom risotto you will ever make, as testified by my photographer Laura and her husband Bob who, on eating it, instantly added it to his last meal list.

ROAST CHICKEN + MUSHROOM RISOTTO

SERVES **4**

30 MINUTES TO MAKE

30 MINUTES TO COOK

2 TABLESPOONS OLIVE OIL

1 SMALL ONION OR 2 BANANA
SHALLOTS, FINELY SLICED

350G RISOTTO RICE

200ML WHITE WINE OR VERMOUTH
OR VODKA

500-700ML HOT CHICKEN STOCK
(HOMEMADE STOCK – PAGE 19 –
OR A PORCINI STOCK CUBE IS
GREAT)

50G UNSALTED BUTTER

350G BUTTON, CHESTNUT OR FLAT
MUSHROOMS, FINELY CHOPPED

150ML DOUBLE CREAM OR CRÈME
FRAÎCHE

SEA SALT AND FRESHLY GROUND BLACK
PEPPER

ABOUT 200-300G LEFTOVER ROAST
CHICKEN, SHREDDED, PLUS ANY
LEFTOVER GRAVY (PAGE 19)

30G PARMESAN CHEESE, GRATED

A HANDFUL OF FINELY CHOPPED
FLAT-LEAF PARSLEY

1. Heat the oil in a saucepan and gently fry the onion for 5–10 minutes until softened but not too coloured. Add the rice and toast in the oil and onion for 30 seconds until the grains become slightly translucent.

2. Splosh in the wine and stir vigorously until it is all absorbed. Then start adding your stock, a ladleful at a time, stirring and making sure each addition is absorbed before adding the next.

3. Meanwhile, melt the butter in a frying pan and fry the chopped mushrooms over a medium–high heat until golden brown. Add the cream or crème fraîche and season with sea salt and black pepper and bubble together then whizz in a blender or mini processor until you have a paste.

4. Once the rice is almost cooked, add the mushroom paste and a little more seasoning to taste and stir in. Add a good ladleful of stock, the chicken and Parmesan and remove from the heat. Cover with a lid and leave it to stand for 5 minutes – this relaxes the rice and lets it become unctuous and silky. Add the parsley and serve.

tip If you haven't cooked the Roast Chicken with Lemon + Tarragon (page 19), you can roast 250g chicken (breast, thigh or leg) in a hot oven (200°C/fan 180°C/gas 6) for 20 minutes while you cook the risotto and use this for the finished dish.

Anything goes in this super speedy midweek supper – whatever vegetables and bits and pieces you have in your fridge and left over from your roast chicken will work brilliantly.

QUICK CHICKEN, PURPLE SPROUTING BROCCOLI + STICKY CHILLI STIR-FRY

SERVES 4
10 MINUTES TO MAKE
10 MINUTES TO COOK

2 TABLESPOONS SUNFLOWER OR
  VEGETABLE OIL
2 GARLIC CLOVES, SLICED
2.5CM PIECE OF FRESH GINGER,
  PEELED AND FINELY SLICED
  INTO MATCHSTICKS
1-2 RED CHILLIES, FINELY SLICED
STAR ANISE
300G PURPLE SPROUTING BROCCOLI
  OR ANY OTHER GREENS, SUCH AS
  CABBAGE, PAK CHOI, CAVALO NERO
  OR CHINESE LEAF
ABOUT 200-300G LEFTOVER ROAST
  CHICKEN (PAGE 19), CHOPPED
100-200G LEFTOVER ROAST POTATOES
  (PAGE 19), SLICED
1 TABLESPOON RICE WINE VINEGAR
2 TABLESPOONS RUNNY HONEY OR
  SWEET CHILLI DIPPING SAUCE
2 TABLESPOONS DARK OR LIGHT SOY
  SAUCE
A BIG HANDFUL OF CORIANDER,
  ROUGHLY CHOPPED
LIME WEDGES AND RICE, TO SERVE

1. Heat the oil in a wok or large frying pan over a high heat and very quickly speed-fry the garlic, ginger and chillies for 30 seconds. Add the star anise, broccoli and a splash of water (about 1–2 tablespoons) and cook in the steam, tossing gently for 2–3 minutes. Add the remaining ingredients except for the coriander.

2. Cook for a minute, tossing until coated in sticky sauce, then add the coriander and serve with rice and lime wedges.

tip If you haven't cooked the Roast Chicken with Lemon + Tarragon (page 19), use 2 chicken breasts or 4 thighs, meat sliced and stir-fry quickly for 5–6 minutes at the start of the recipe.

I love the versatility of koftes, whether eaten simply with yogurt and herbs in a wrap, with a grain or cooked in a sauce, or even on the barbecue, they always hit the spot.

LAMB KOFTES WITH MINT + YOGURT

SERVES **4**, PLUS LEFTOVERS
30 MINUTES TO MAKE
20 MINUTES TO COOK

1½ TEASPOONS FENNEL SEEDS

1½ TEASPOONS CORIANDER SEEDS

3 TEASPOONS CUMIN SEEDS

GOOD PINCH OF CHILLI POWDER

1KG LAMB MINCE

1 SMALL BUNCH OF MINT, FINELY
  CHOPPED

FINELY GRATED ZEST AND JUICE OF
  1 LEMON

300G COUSCOUS OR BULGAR WHEAT

450ML HOT CHICKEN STOCK (PAGE 19
  FOR HOMEMADE)

1 TABLESPOON OLIVE OIL

SEA SALT AND FRESHLY GROUND BLACK
  PEPPER

1 RED ONION, FINELY SLICED

250G GREEK YOGURT

1 GARLIC CLOVE, CRUSHED

½ CUCUMBER, DICED

A HANDFUL CORIANDER, ROUGHLY
  CHOPPED, TO SERVE

1. Dry-fry the spices in a saucepan until they smell fragrant then roughly crush in a pestle and mortar. Mix the lamb mince with the spices and half the mint. Season well and add the lemon zest. With wet hands shape into 28 small koftes. Chill for 30 minutes.

2. Put the couscous in a saucepan and pour over the hot stock. Bring to the boil then remove from the heat, cover and leave to stand for 10 minutes until the stock is absorbed. Tip into a bowl and add half the lemon juice, a glug of olive oil and season. Squeeze the remaining lemon juice over the red onion, season and set aside.

3. Heat the oil in a frying pan and fry the koftes until golden brown and cooked through – about 10 minutes. Set one third aside for leftovers and keep the remainder warm in a low oven at 120°C/fan 100°C/gas ½.

4. Mix the Greek yogurt with the garlic, cucumber and remaining mint and season well. Serve the kofte with the couscous, dollop over the yogurt and scatter with the red onion and coriander.

tip Try making these koftes with turkey or chicken mince instead of lamb.

ENOUGH LEFT OVER FOR:
SPICED LAMB + HUMMUS WRAPS (PAGE 24)
SORT OF MOUSSAKA (PAGE 25)➙⟶

Somehow a wrap is so much more than just a sandwich, their pocket-like nature means you can stuff them to the gills with all sorts of yumminess. Add anything you like to these – sliced peppers, griddled aubergine or courgette, feta cheese – whatever you have in your fridge that takes your fancy.

SERVES **4**
10 MINUTES TO MAKE
15 MINUTES TO COOK

SPICED LAMB + HUMMUS WRAPS

1 TABLESPOON OLIVE OIL, PLUS A GLUG
   FOR THE HUMMUS

1 RED ONION, FINELY SLICED

250G LEFTOVER LAMB KOFTES (PAGE 23)

400G CAN OF CHICKPEAS, DRAINED
   AND RINSED

1-2 TABLESPOONS TAHINI

2 GARLIC CLOVES, CRUSHED

GOOD PINCH OF PAPRIKA

JUICE OF 1 LEMON

SEA SALT AND FRESHLY GROUND BLACK
   PEPPER

4 SOFT FLOUR TORTILLAS

YOGURT, TO SERVE

SEVERAL HANDFULS OF BABY LEAVES,
   SUCH AS ROCKET, WATERCRESS, PEA
   SHOOTS, BABY BEET OR LITTLE GEM
   HEARTS, TO SERVE

1. Heat the oil in a pan and gently fry the onion for 10 minutes until soft. Break up the kofte and fry until warmed. Set aside.

2. In a food processor, blitz the chickpeas with the tahini, garlic, paprika and olive oil and enough lemon juice to sharpen. Loosen with a little water and season.

3. Wrap the tortillas in foil and warm in a low oven then dollop on a good amount of the hummus, a dollop of yogurt then top with the lamb and some baby leaves. Wrap and eat.

tip If you haven't cooked the Lamb Koftes on page 23 then fry 200g lamb mince in a little olive oil over a high heat with a ½ teaspoon each of fennel and cumin seeds for 10–12 minutes.

This is a great cheaty version of a moussaka using Greek yogurt for the topping but somehow it is even more delicious for having to do so little work.

SERVES **4**
20 MINUTES TO MAKE
50 MINUTES TO COOK

SORT OF MOUSSAKA

OLIVE OIL, TO FRY

1 LARGE ONION, FINELY SLICED

400G LEFTOVER LAMB KOFTES
(PAGE 23), CHOPPED

400G CAN OF CHOPPED TOMATOES

1 TABLESPOON TOMATO PURÉE

A FEW SPRIGS OF OREGANO, LEAVES
STRIPPED

SEA SALT AND FRESHLY GROUND BLACK
PEPPER

3 LARGE AUBERGINES, SLICED

400G GREEK YOGURT

3 FREE-RANGE EGGS

250G FETA CHEESE OR OTHER
CRUMBLY CHEESE, SUCH AS
WENSLEYDALE, CRUMBLED

GREEN SALAD, TO SERVE

1. Preheat the oven to 200°C/fan 180°C/gas 6. Heat a drizzle of oil in a frying pan and gently fry the onion for 10 minutes. Add the chopped kofte, tomatoes and tomato purée. Scatter in the oregano and a splash of water, season and simmer gently for 10–15 minutes.

2. Meanwhile, heat a good layer of oil in a non-stick frying pan and fry the slices of aubergine in batches for 10 minutes until coloured and softened. In a 1.8–2-litre ovenproof dish, layer up the aubergine with the kofte mixture.

3. Mix together the yogurt with the eggs and cheese and pour over the top of the dish. Bake for 45–50 minutes until the topping is golden and puffed up. Serve immediately with a green salad.

tip If you haven't cooked the Lamb Koftes (page 23), then fry 200g lamb mince for 10 minutes until browned all over instead.

Shoulder of lamb is one of the best slow-roasting joints as the fat and sinews melt into the meat until it is so soft you can shred it with a fork. The barbecue is a greatly underused bit of kit and if you get the hang of using it for slow cooking you will be out there in the depths of winter armed with your tongs and charcoal.

CHARGRILLED LAMB SHOULDER

SERVES 4–6, PLUS LEFTOVERS
15 MINUTES TO MAKE
2–2½ HOURS TO COOK

1 LARGE SHOULDER OF LAMB,
   WEIGHING ABOUT 2–2.5KG
500G GREEK YOGURT
4 GARLIC CLOVES, CRUSHED
4 SPRIGS OF ROSEMARY, LEAVES
   STRIPPED AND FINELY CHOPPED
3 ANCHOVIES, FINELY CHOPPED
FINELY GRATED ZEST AND JUICE OF
   1 LEMON
1 TABLESPOON SOFT BROWN SUGAR
SEA SALT AND FRESHLY GROUND BLACK
   PEPPER

1. Put the lamb shoulder in a dish and make incisions all over it with a sharp knife.

2. Mix the yogurt with the remaining ingredients and season well. Spread all over the lamb and leave to marinate for at least an hour or overnight if possible.

3. Light a kettle barbecue and get it nice and hot. Put the lamb on the barbecue and char the lamb on each side for 5–10 minutes. Transfer to a roasting tin lined with a large double layer of foil and pour in 200ml water. Bring the foil around to enclose the lamb then return to the barbecue and shut the lid. Cook for 2 hours, checking every so often and topping up with more water if it is drying out, until the meat is tender and falling from the bone.

tip This recipe is ideal to cook on a barbecue but if you fancy doing it in the oven it is really simple. Just roast in a roasting tin lined with foil as above for 2½ hours at 160°C/fan 140°C/gas 3. Then uncover and increase the temperature to 220°C/fan 200°C/gas 7 and brown for 15 minutes.

ENOUGH LEFT OVER FOR:
LAMB KARAHI (PAGE 28)
FATTEH (PAGE 30) »——→

A great simple curry to have at your fingertips, fast and no-nonsense, this always hits the spot. These flavours would be great with chicken or you could make this veggie by adding chickpeas instead of lamb.

SERVES **4**
10 MINUTES TO MAKE
30–40 MINUTES TO COOK

LAMB KARAHI

4 TABLESPOONS OLIVE OIL

2 AUBERGINES, CUT INTO CUBES

GOOD KNOB OF BUTTER

1 ONION, SLICED

2 GARLIC CLOVES, FINELY SLICED

2 TEASPOONS CUMIN SEEDS

2 TEASPOONS GROUND CORIANDER

1 TEASPOON GROUND TURMERIC

2 DRIED RED CHILLIES OR 1 TEASPOON
   CHILLI FLAKES

400G CAN OF CHOPPED TOMATOES

400G LEFTOVER CHARGRILLED
   LAMB SHOULDER (PAGE 27),
   SHREDDED

SEA SALT AND FRESHLY GROUND BLACK
   PEPPER

1 TEASPOON GARAM MARSALA

1. Heat the oil in a saucepan and gently fry the aubergines for 10–15 minutes until really soft. Set aside. Add the butter to the pan and gently fry the onion for 10 minutes until softened. Add the garlic and spices and fry for a further minute.

2. Add the tomatoes, lamb and cooked aubergines with a good splash of water and plenty of seasoning and bubble for 15–20 minutes then add the garam masala. Serve with rice.

tip If you haven't cooked the Chargrilled Lamb Shoulder (page 27), use 400g diced lamb leg steaks in step 2.

Meaning 'to crumble' in Arabic, fatteh is stale or toasted bread, crumbled and layered with other ingredients. A bit like the best Middle Eastern nacho dish you could imagine. Sweet tomatoes, richly spiced leftover lamb and lots of yogurt create a sumptuous leftovers dinner from almost entirely store cupboard ingredients.

SERVES 4
25 MINUTES TO MAKE
45–50 MINUTES TO COOK

FATTEH

2 TABLESPOONS OLIVE OIL

1 LARGE ONION, FINELY SLICED

3 GARLIC CLOVES, CRUSHED

1 CINNAMON STICK

1 TEASPOON PAPRIKA

400G CAN OF CHOPPED TOMATOES

400G LEFTOVER CHARGRILLED LAMB
   SHOULDER (PAGE 27), SHREDDED

SEA SALT AND FRESHLY GROUND BLACK
   PEPPER

6 WHITE PITTA BREADS, OPENED OUT

25G UNSALTED BUTTER, MELTED

250ML GREEK YOGURT OR NATURAL
   YOGURT

50G TOASTED PINE NUTS

A HANDFUL OF CHOPPED CORIANDER,
   TO SCATTER

FOR THE RICE

GOOD KNOB OF UNSALTED BUTTER

1 ONION, FINELY CHOPPED

150G BASMATI RICE

400G CAN OF CHICKPEAS, DRAINED
   AND RINSED

50G SULTANAS

1. Heat the oil in a saucepan and gently fry the onion for 10 minutes. Add the garlic, cinnamon stick and paprika and cook for a minute then add the tomatoes and lamb. Season and bubble for 15 minutes until thickened.

2. Meanwhile, for the rice, melt the butter in a pan, add the onion and fry gently for 10 minutes until softened. Add the rice and stir to coat then add the chickpeas and sultanas and 300ml water. Season and cover and simmer gently for 10–12 minutes until the rice is tender.

3. Brush the pitta breads with melted butter and cut into triangles. Toast in a medium oven at 160°C/fan 140°C/gas 3 until golden and crisp.

4. Place the pitta breads on a platter and top with the rice, then spoon over the lamb mixture and finish with some dollops of yogurt, the toasted pine nuts and a scattering of coriander.

tip If you haven't made the Chargrilled Lamb Shoulder (page 27), then use 400g lamb mince and cook it with the onion and spices at the start of the recipe until tender. It has a slightly different texture but is just as delicious.

Somehow people always seem to be a bit scared of lamb racks – that they are either too smart or too difficult for a normal supper. If you think about them as small lamb chops you will find them instantly more accessible. The great thing about a rack of lamb is that you get lots of the lovely pink meat when you cook them as a whole.

SERVES 4, PLUS LEFTOVERS
15 MINUTES TO MAKE
25 MINUTES TO COOK

2 X 6 BONE RACKS OF LAMB
1 TABLESPOON SEA SALT
FRESHLY GROUND BLACK PEPPER
A HANDFUL OF THYME SPRIGS,
    LEAVES STRIPPED
OLIVE OIL, TO DRIZZLE

FOR THE SALSA VERDE
1 SMALL BUNCH EACH OF MINT
    AND BASIL LEAVES, TOUGH STALKS
    REMOVED
1 BIG BUNCH OF FLAT-LEAF PARSLEY
2 TABLESPOONS CAPERS, RINSED
6-8 ANCHOVY FILLETS, CHOPPED
75-100ML OLIVE OIL
LEMON JUICE, TO TASTE

SALT-CRUSTED LAMB RACKS WITH SALSA VERDE

1. Preheat the oven to 220°C/fan 200°C/gas 7. Trim the skin from the lamb and score the fat with a sharp knife. Mix the salt with plenty of pepper and the thyme and a small splash of water and press onto the outside of the racks. Drizzle with oil and put into a roasting tin and roast for 20-25 minutes for a nice pink middle.

2. Meanwhile, chop the herbs for the salsa verde as finely as possible and mix with the remaining ingredients. Add a small splash of water to loosen if necessary.

3. Rest the lamb racks for 10 minutes then slice and serve with the salsa verde.

tip Cooking 2 racks of lamb will leave plenty for leftovers for the next day or the day after based on 2 chops per person for the main recipe.

ENOUGH LEFT OVER FOR:
WARM LAMB + WATERCRESS SALAD (PAGE 32)
QUICK LAMB PIZZAIOLA (PAGE 33) »——→

Cold lamb can be a bit fatty so it is best to heat it up a little first, which makes it perfect for a robust warm salad. Feel free to add in other ingredients such as capers or olives or finely sliced preserved lemons.

WARM LAMB + WATERCRESS SALAD

SERVES **4**

15 MINUTES TO MAKE

15 MINUTES TO COOK

300G NEW POTATOES

2 COURGETTES

100G FROZEN PEAS, DEFROSTED

3-4 LEFTOVER SALT-CRUSTED LAMB
    RACKS (PAGE 31), SLICED (ABOUT 200G
    MEAT)

100G WATERCRESS, ROCKET, LAMB'S
    LETTUCE OR OTHER LEAVES

30G PARMESAN SHAVINGS

JUICE OF ½ LEMON

SEA SALT AND FRESHLY GROUND BLACK
    PEPPER

PINCH OF CASTER SUGAR

2 TEASPOONS DIJON MUSTARD

3-4 TABLESPOONS EXTRA VIRGIN
    OLIVE OIL

1. Put the potatoes in a pan of cold salted water, bring to the boil and simmer for 10–12 minutes until tender. Drain and halve then tip into a salad bowl.

2. Use a potato peeler to shave the courgettes into the bowl in long ribbons, add the peas, lamb and watercress and toss together. Scatter with the Parmesan shavings.

3. Whisk the lemon with a good pinch of salt and pepper and a little bit of sugar and the mustard. When blended, drizzle in the oil, whisking until you have a glossy dressing. Pour over the salad, toss together and serve.

tip If you haven't cooked the Salt-crusted Lamb Racks (page 31), simply pan-fry 1–2 seasoned lamb neck fillets in a drizzle of olive oil until browned then cook in the oven at 200°C/180°C fan/gas 6 for 5–6 minutes until cooked but still pink in the middle.

A great thing about leftovers is making quick versions of dishes that normally take a long time, as you have done so much of the work already. This is a great supper standby. The anchovies are optional, but do try it with them, they melt into the sauce and give a lovely background flavour without being in the slightest bit fishy.

SERVES **2** OR **4** AS A LIGHT LUNCH
5 MINUTES TO MAKE
15 MINUTES TO COOK

QUICK LAMB PIZZAIOLA

75ML EXTRA VIRGIN OLIVE OIL

2 GARLIC CLOVES, FINELY SLICED

2-3 ANCHOVIES, CHOPPED

600G VINE TOMATOES, ROUGHLY
 CHOPPED OR 400G CAN OF
 CHOPPED TOMATOES

1 TEASPOON RED WINE VINEGAR

FEW SPRIGS OF OREGANO OR
 THYME LEAVES STRIPPED

1 TABLESPOON CAPERS, RINSED

SEA SALT AND FRESHLY GROUND
 BLACK PEPPER

A LARGE HANDFUL OF ROCKET LEAVES

3-4 LEFTOVER SALT-CRUSTED LAMB
 RACKS (PAGE 31), SLICED (ABOUT
 150-200G MEAT)

PARMESAN SHAVINGS AND CRUSTY
 BREAD, TO SERVE

1. Heat the oil in a pan over a medium heat and add the garlic and anchovies and cook for 30 seconds then add the tomatoes, vinegar, oregano and capers and season. Cook for about 15 minutes until the tomatoes are softened and starting to break down.

2. Spoon the tomato onto warmed plates, top with some rocket, slices of the lamb and Parmesan shavings. Drizzle with extra virgin olive oil and serve with crusty bread.

tip If you haven't cooked the Salt-crusted Lamb Racks (page 31), pan-fry 200g lamb leg steaks in a drizzle of olive oil for 2-3 minutes each side until just cooked then slice.

Rump cap, or *picanha* as it is known in Brazil, is still a little known cut over here. It is the cap of meat that normally sits on top of the whole rump – you get a little bit of it when you buy rump steak. Instead of slicing as part of the rump, it is removed and sold as a whole piece. It is like a steak roasting joint, meaning you get the best of both worlds.

SPICE-CRUSTED RUMP CAP WITH PUY LENTIL SALAD

SERVES **4**, PLUS LEFTOVERS
15 MINUTES TO MAKE
35 MINUTES TO COOK

2 TEASPOONS BLACK PEPPERCORNS

2 TEASPOONS SEA SALT

2 TEASPOONS CUMIN SEEDS

1 TEASPOON CORIANDER SEEDS

GOOD GRATING OF NUTMEG

PINCH OF CHILLI FLAKES

1.5KG WHOLE RUMP CAP

OLIVE OIL, TO DRIZZLE

FOR THE LENTILS

300G PUY LENTILS

600ML CHICKEN STOCK (PAGE 19)

1 SWEET ONION, FINELY SLICED

1 TABLESPOON CIDER VINEGAR

3 TABLESPOONS EXTRA VIRGIN
 OLIVE OIL

A HANDFUL OF FLAT-LEAF PARSLEY,
 CHOPPED

1. Preheat the oven to 200°C/fan 180°C/gas 6. Mix the pepper, salt and spices together in a pestle and mortar and pound to a coarse mixture. Heat a heavy-based pan over a high heat, drizzle the beef with olive oil and sear briefly on all sides until golden. Press the spice crust all over the beef and put it in a roasting tin and roast for 30–35 minutes until cooked but still pink inside – it should read 50–52°C on a digital thermometer. Leave it to rest for at least 10 minutes before serving.

2. Meanwhile, put the lentils in a pan with the stock, season and bring to the boil. Simmer for 15–20 minutes until tender and the stock is absorbed. Drain any excess stock and tip the lentils into a bowl. Toss with the sweet onion. Mix the cider vinegar with plenty of salt and pepper then whisk in the olive oil to make a glossy dressing. Pour over the lentils and toss together with the parsley. Serve with slices of rump cap.

tip If you can't get hold of a whole rump cap you can easily use a whole piece of sirloin steak instead, imagine 4–5 nice fat steaks together in a piece and you should have the right amount.

ENOUGH LEFT OVER FOR:
TAGLIATA (PAGE 36)
BEEF WITH BÉARNAISE SAUCE + CHIPS (PAGE 38) »⟶

If I am honest I do love cold steak or roast beef on its own, with a smidge of mustard, but sometimes it's fun to mix things up and create something a bit more special. It doesn't take much to turn leftover steak into something fabulous like this tagliata.

SERVES **4**
5 MINUTES TO MAKE
2–3 MINUTES TO COOK

200G WILD ROCKET, WATERCRESS OR
   OTHER SPICY SALAD LEAVES
300G LEFTOVER SPICE-CRUSTED RUMP
   CAP (PAGE 35), THINLY SLICED
120ML EXTRA VIRGIN OLIVE OIL
2 SPRIGS OF ROSEMARY
1 LARGE GARLIC CLOVE, BASHED
PARED ZEST OF ½ LEMON, PLUS JUICE
   OF 1 LEMON
PARMESAN SHAVINGS, TO SERVE

TAGLIATA

1. Put the rocket into a salad bowl and place the sliced beef on top.

2. Heat the oil in a pan over a very low heat and add the rosemary, garlic and lemon zest and leave to infuse for a couple of minutes. Remove from the heat and whisk in the lemon juice.

3. Spoon the dressing over the steak and leaves, scatter with Parmesan and serve.

tip If you haven't cooked the Spice-crusted Rump Cap (page 35), then rub 2 x 150g rump or sirloin steaks in a little olive oil and sear for 1–2 minutes on each side until rare before you make the dressing.

Something as simple as a béarnaise sauce and really good chips can transform leftover steak or roast beef into something sumptuous. Don't be afraid of Béarnaise sauce, this method is as easy as any I've ever tried.

BEEF WITH BÉARNAISE SAUCE + CHIPS

SERVES 4
30 MINUTES TO MAKE
50 MINUTES TO COOK

800G FLOURY POTATOES, SUCH KING EDWARD OR MARIS PIPER
40G DRIPPING OR 3 TABLESPOONS OLIVE OIL
400G LEFTOVER SPICE-CRUSTED RUMP CAP (PAGE 35)

FOR THE BÉARNAISE
2 TABLESPOONS WHITE WINE VINEGAR
6 BLACK PEPPERCORNS
1 SHALLOT, FINELY CHOPPED
1 BUNCH OF TARRAGON, LEAVES STRIPPED AND CHOPPED, STALKS RESERVED
2 FREE-RANGE EGG YOLKS
SEA SALT AND FRESHLY GROUND BLACK PEPPER
220G COLD UNSALTED BUTTER, CUT INTO CUBES
LEMON JUICE, TO TASTE

1. Preheat the oven to 200°C/fan 180°C/gas 6. Peel the potatoes and cut into whatever size and shape chips you like – I love little cubes so you get extra golden crunchy bits. Drop into a pan of cold, salted water, bring to the boil and simmer for 3–5 minutes (depending on size) until parboiled. Drain and return to the pan over a low heat and toss gently to fluff up the edges.

2. Heat the dripping or oil in a roasting tin then add the potatoes and toss to coat. Roast for 45–50 minutes, turning occasionally, until gorgeously golden and crisp.

3. Meanwhile, put the vinegar and 1 tablespoon of water into a small pan over a medium heat. Add the peppercorns, shallot and the tarragon stalks. Bubble until reduced to 2 teaspoons in volume. Sieve into a medium heatproof bowl.

4. Place the bowl over a pan of barely simmering water so the bottom doesn't touch the water. Add the egg yolks to the vinegar with some seasoning and whisk for 30 seconds. Gradually add the butter cubes, whisking all the time, allowing them to melt and become emulsified before adding the next couple. Keep going until you have used up all the butter and you have a glossy thick sauce. Remove from the pan and keep whisking as you add the chopped tarragon and lemon juice to taste.

5. Remove the rump cap from the fridge 20 minutes before serving, slice and serve with the chips and Béarnaise sauce.

tip If you haven't cooked the Spice-crusted Rump Cap (page 35), sear 2 x 200g sirloin or rump steaks in a drizzle of olive oil for 1–2 minutes each side.

On a cold day there is nothing as lovely as a big plateful of a rich meaty ragù. For me, beef shin has to be my favourite choice for a slow braise as its gelatinous nature adds a depth to the gravy that you just don't get with other cuts.

SLOW-COOKED BEEF RAGÙ

SERVES **4–6**, PLUS LEFTOVERS
30 MINUTES TO MAKE
3 HOURS TO COOK

OLIVE OIL, TO FRY

SEA SALT AND FRESHLY GROUND BLACK
  PEPPER

4 TABLESPOONS PLAIN FLOUR

1.5KG SHIN OF BEEF, CUT INTO LARGE
  2-3CM CHUNKS

150G COOKING CHORIZO, CUT INTO
  1CM PIECES

1 ONION, FINELY SLICED

1 CARROT, FINELY CHOPPED

2 STICKS CELERY, FINELY CHOPPED

2 BAY LEAVES

6 SPRIGS OF THYME

300ML WHITE WINE

400G TIN CHOPPED TOMATOES

2 TABLESPOONS TOMATO PURÉE, PLUS
  A SQUIDGE EXTRA

300ML FRESH BEEF OR CHICKEN STOCK
  (PAGE 19)

2 TEASPOONS SOFT LIGHT BROWN
  SUGAR

1. Take a large flameproof casserole dish and heat the oil in the bottom. Season the flour, toss the chunks of beef in it and brown in batches in the hot oil then remove with a slotted spoon. Once the beef is browned, add the chorizo and brown all over.

2. Remove all but a couple of tablespoons of the oil from the casserole then add the onion, carrot and celery and fry gently for 10 minutes. Return the meat to the pan and add the herbs and white wine. Bubble for a few minutes then add the tomatoes, tomato purée, stock and sugar. Season and bring to the boil. Cover and reduce to a simmer and cook for 2–2½ hours until really tender and falling apart. Remove the lid for the last 45 minutes of cooking to reduce the sauce to a thick, glossy gravy.

ENOUGH LEFT OVER FOR:
BEEF + BARLEY SOUP (PAGE 42)
SMOKY BEEF EMPANADAS (PAGE 43) »——→

A great way of using up leftover braises, stews and ragùs is to turn them into soup. The beauty is they are halfway there already. A little more stock and few extra ingredients can transform last night's supper into a wonderful winter lunch.

BEEF + BARLEY SOUP

1 TABLESPOON OLIVE OIL

1 LARGE ONION, FINELY CHOPPED

A WHOLE SPRIG OF ROSEMARY

ABOUT 400G LEFTOVER SLOW-COOKED BEEF RAGÙ (PAGE 39)

1 LITRE BEEF STOCK (FRESH IS BEST OR FROM A CUBE)

150G PEARL BARLEY

CRUSTY BREAD, TO SERVE

1. Heat the oil in a deep pan and gently fry the onion and rosemary for 10 minutes until lovely and soft. Add your leftover beef ragù, the stock and pearl barley and cook gently for 30–40 minutes until the pearl barley is cooked and tender. Serve with hunks of crusty bread.

tip If you haven't made the Slow-cooked Beef Ragù (page 39), don't worry, you can still make this wonderful soup. Brown off 300g braising steak. Add ½ teaspoon each smoked hot and sweet paprika to the frying onions then add the steak and stock with a squidge of tomato purée and a small tin of chopped tomatoes and simmer gently for 30 minutes before adding the barley and another slosh of beef stock. Simmer for a further 30–45 minutes until the barley is tender.

The pasty of the Spanish-speaking world, empanadas are great as a portable lunch or as a great leftovers supper with a big green salad.

SMOKY BEEF EMPANADAS

MAKES **6**
40 MINUTES TO MAKE
25–30 MINUTES TO COOK

FOR THE FILLING
1 TABLESPOON OLIVE OIL
1 LARGE ONION, FINELY SLICED
2 TEASPOONS SMOKED PAPRIKA
ABOUT 300G LEFTOVER SLOW-COOKED
    BEEF RAGÙ (PAGE 39)
200G FROZEN PEAS, DEFROSTED
2–3 TABLESPOONS SOURED CREAM,
    GREEK YOGURT OR CRÈME FRAÎCHE

FOR THE PASTRY
250G PLAIN FLOUR
½ TEASPOON FINE SALT
100G COLD UNSALTED BUTTER, CUBED
1 FREE-RANGE EGG, BEATEN
1 TEASPOON WHITE WINE VINEGAR

tip If you haven't made the Slow-cooked Beef Ragù (page 39), add 300g beef mince to the frying onion and brown. Add 1 teaspoon of paprika, a small can of tomatoes and a splash of beef stock. Simmer for 30 minutes until thickened then add the peas and soured cream and leave to cool.

1. To make the pastry, tip the flour and salt into a bowl and rub the cold butter into it with your fingers until it resembles breadcrumbs. Mix half the beaten egg with 2 tablespoons of cold water and vinegar, add to the bowl and mix in quickly. Bring together with your hands and knead very briefly to make a smooth dough. Shape into a disc, wrap in clingfilm and chill for at least 30 minutes.

2. For the filling, heat the oil in a pan and gently fry the onion for 10 minutes. Add the paprika and cook for 30 seconds then add the leftover ragù and peas and cook for 10 minutes, breaking the pieces of beef up with a wooden spoon. Spread onto a tray to cool. Mix in the soured cream, yogurt or crème fraîche.

3. Divide the pastry into 6 even-sized pieces and roll into balls. Roll each ball out into a disc and use a cutter or small plate to cut them into circles 16cm in diameter. Discard any trimmings.

4. Preheat the oven to 200°C/fan 180°C/gas 6. Cover all but one of the discs with a slightly damp tea towel to stop them drying out. Spoon a dollop of the mixture into the centre of the uncovered pastry circle then brush the edges with a little water and fold them in half to enclose the filling in a semicircle. Press the edges to seal and crimp with your fingers or a fork.

5. Place on a baking sheet lined with baking parchment and repeat with the remaining pastry and filling. Then brush with the remaining beaten egg and bake for 25–30 minutes until golden brown. Serve warm or at room temperature.

Boy, oh boy are these ribs the dawg's proverbials! With so little effort required on your part to make these amazing beauties it's almost embarrassing! I'd go so far as to say this might be the best rib recipe I have ever written.

STICKY BRAISED SHORT RIBS

SERVES **4**, PLUS LEFTOVERS
20 MINUTES TO MAKE
4 HOURS TO COOK

2KG BEEF SHORT RIBS
200ML LIGHT SOY SAUCE
200ML DARK SOY SAUCE
300G SOFT LIGHT BROWN SUGAR
A GOOD SQUIDGE OF RUNNY HONEY
6 GARLIC CLOVES, BASHED
5CM PIECE OF FRESH GINGER,
    PEELED AND SLICED
2 STAR ANISE
2 RED CHILLIES, FINELY SLICED
4 TABLESPOONS RICE WINE VINEGAR

1. Put the ribs into a shallow, non-metallic dish. Mix the soy sauces with 250g of the sugar, honey, garlic, ginger, star anise and chillies and pour over the ribs. Marinate in the fridge for at least 3 hours or overnight if possible.

2. Preheat the oven to 160°C/fan 140°C/gas 3. Transfer the ribs and their marinade to a roasting tin, cover with foil and roast for 3–4 hours until the meat is very tender and falling off the bone. Check on them every so often and add a splash of water if they are getting dry. At this point you can leave the ribs to cool in the marinade and finish the next day.

3. When ready to finish, preheat the oven to 200°C/fan 180°C/gas 6. Pour off the marinade into a pan, add the rice wine vinegar and the remaining sugar and bubble to thicken to a glossy glaze. Put the ribs into the oven with a good drizzle of the glaze and roast, glazing and turning every 10 minutes, for 30 minutes or so until you have sticky rich and sexy ribs. Serve with any leftover glaze.

ENOUGH LEFT OVER FOR:
THAI BEEF SALAD (PAGE 46)
BEEF SUMMER ROLLS (PAGE 48) »——→

Big, bold and beautiful, this is a salad to remember. Rather than the usual rare steak I thought that using leftover sticky sweet rib meat would be perfect in such a zing-filled salad, and I was right!

SERVES **4**

15 MINUTES TO MAKE

1 CUCUMBER

2 CARROTS

100G RADISHES

150G MANGE TOUT, SUGAR SNAPS OR
PEAS

100G CHERRY TOMATOES, QUARTERED

½ BUNCH OF SPRING ONIONS, FINELY
SLICED

2 BABY GEM OR OTHER CRUNCHY
LETTUCES

1 SMALL BUNCH OF CORIANDER,
ROUGHLY CHOPPED

250-300G LEFTOVER STICKY
BRAISED SHORT RIBS (PAGE 45),
MEAT SHREDDED

2 TABLESPOONS SALTED PEANUTS,
CHOPPED

FOR THE DRESSING

JUICE OF 2 LIMES

1 TABLESPOON FISH SAUCE

1 TABLESPOON DARK OR LIGHT SOY
SAUCE

2 TEASPOONS SOFT BROWN SUGAR OR
PALM SUGAR

1 RED CHILLI, FINELY SLICED

2 TABLESPOONS SESAME OIL

THAI BEEF SALAD

1. Use a potato peeler to slice the cucumber and carrots into ribbons (or you can julienne the carrots if you prefer). Finely slice the radishes and mange tout or sugar snaps and toss together in a big bowl with the cherry tomatoes and spring onions.

2. Cut the baby gem into wedges and toss with the salad. Scatter over the coriander and shredded beef.

3. Mix all the ingredients for the dressing together in a small bowl and pour over the top of the salad, scatter with the peanuts and serve immediately.

tip If you haven't cooked the Sticky Braised Short Ribs (page 45), you can sear a 200–250g sirloin steak over a high heat for 1–2 minutes each side. Mix 3 tablespoons of dark or light soy sauce with 1 tablespoon of soft light brown sugar, 1 tablespoon of rice wine vinegar and 1 chopped chilli together in a saucepan over a medium heat and bubble until slightly thickened. Slice the beef and pour over the sauce and leave to stand while you make the salad.

These fresh and vibrant summer rolls are a great dish to make for friends, they look really impressive but actually are so simple and you can prepare them in advance and keep chilled. Every bite is a wonderful burst of flavour.

BEEF SUMMER ROLLS

100G (1 SLAB) RICE VERMICELLI
 NOODLES OR OTHER RICE NOODLES
16 RICE PAPER WRAPPERS OR
 LETTUCE LEAVES
A HANDFUL OF CORIANDER, LEAVES
 PICKED
A FEW SPRIGS OF MINT, LEAVES
 PICKED
A HANDFUL OF THAI OR PERILLA BASIL,
 LEAVES PICKED
1 CARROT, CUT INTO MATCHSTICKS
½ CUCUMBER, CUT INTO MATCHSTICKS
½ BUTTER LETTUCE, BABY GEM OR
 OTHER LETTUCE, SHREDDED
300G STICKY BRAISED SHORT RIBS
 (PAGE 45), MEAT SHREDDED

FOR THE DIPPING SAUCE
1 TABLESPOON SOFT BROWN SUGAR
JUICE OF 1 LIME
1 TABLESPOON FISH SAUCE
1 GREEN FINGER CHILLI, FINELY SLICED

1. To cook the noodles, put them in a bowl and pour over a kettle full of boiling water and leave for 3–4 minutes until al dente. Drain and run under cold water to stop them cooking then drain well. Set aside.

2. Put the herbs, vegetables, nuts and herbs into small bowls. Have a shallow dish of warm water to soften the rice wrappers and a clean tea towel in front of you on a chopping board.

3. Dip a wrapper in water and when it starts to feel silky and soft, remove it and place on the tea towel. Start with placing a few herbs in a line in the middle of your wrapper, about halfway down. Top this line of herbs with some of each of the remaining ingredients, being careful not to overfill.

4. Fold the the sides in then fold the top down to cover the filling and roll up. You should end up with a layer of herbs along the top of your roll.

5. Repeat until you have used up all the ingredients. Mix the dipping sauce ingredients together in a small bowl and serve straight away.

tip If you haven't cooked the Sticky Braised Short Ribs (page 45), sear 250g sirloin steak for 1-2 minutes each side until medium rare. Rest for 5 minutes then slice thinly.

An almost magical transformation occurs when you slow cook pork until the tender shreds of meat fall apart, full of flavour and silky smooth to eat, hardly a tooth is required except for the crackling. But it's the crackling that seals the deal making this a truly great roast.

SLOW-ROAST JUNIPER + FENNEL SEED PORK BELLY

SERVES 4–6, PLUS LEFTOVERS
15 MINUTES TO MAKE
5 HOURS TO COOK

3-4KG PIECE OF OUTDOOR-REARED
    PORK BELLY, RIBS REMOVED BUT
    RETAINED AND SKIN SCORED
3 RED ONIONS, CUT INTO THIN
    WEDGES
2 TEASPOONS JUNIPER BERRIES,
    ROUGHLY CRUSHED
DRIZZLE OF OLIVE OIL
1 TABLESPOON SEA SALT FLAKES
1 TABLESPOON GREEN FENNEL SEEDS
300ML DRY CIDER

1. Preheat the oven to 220°C/fan 200°C/gas 7. Put the ribs of the pork belly into a roasting tin, scatter with the onions and juniper berries and drizzle with a little oil. Use the bones as a trivet for the belly to sit on. Mix the salt with the fennel seeds and press all over the skin.

2. Roast for 30 minutes then reduce the temperature to 150°C/fan 130°C/gas 2 and cook for 4–5 hours until really tender. Increase the temperature to 220°C/fan 200°C/gas 7 for 5–10 minutes to crackle the skin at the end if you need to.

3. Remove from the oven and transfer to a warmed serving plate. Put the roasting tin with the ribs over a low heat and add the cider. Bubble and scrape all the yummy bits from the ribs into the sauce. Serve with the pork belly.

tip Using the ribs as a trivet is a great way to add extra flavour to your gravy, but you also get perfectly slow-cooked ribs as an extra leftover if you don't add them to your gravy. Either eat them cold with a slaw and baked potatoes or you could trim the meat off them to use in other recipes.

ENOUGH LEFT OVER FOR:
GOULASH (PAGE 52)
SHREDDED PORK + APPLE BUNS (PAGE 54) »——→

The beauty of this dish is that all the slow cooking has already been done for you. I've added beetroot to my goulash which isn't traditional, but I love its earthy sweet flavour against the warmth of the spices.

SERVES **4**
10 MINUTES TO MAKE
30 MINUTES TO COOK

2 TABLESPOONS OLIVE OIL

2 ONIONS, FINELY SLICED

2 RED PEPPERS, SLICED

1 TABLESPOON SWEET PAPRIKA

2 TEASPOONS HOT PAPRIKA

2 TEASPOONS CARAWAY SEEDS

GOOD SQUIDGE OF TOMATO PURÉE

500G LEFTOVER SLOW-ROAST JUNIPER
+ FENNEL SEED PORK BELLY,
SHREDDED (PAGE 51)

500ML BEEF STOCK (FRESH IS BEST OR
FROM A CUBE)

300G NEW POTATOES, SWEET
POTATOES OR BUTTERNUT SQUASH,
CHOPPED

3 BEETROOTS, PEELED AND CHOPPED
INTO SMALL PIECES

SOURED CREAM AND CHOPPED
PARSLEY, TO SERVE

GOULASH

1. Heat the oil in a pan and gently fry the onions and peppers for 10 minutes until softened.

2. Add the spices and tomato purée and fry for a further few minutes before adding the pork, stock, potatoes and beetroot. Bring to a simmer and cook for 15–20 minutes until the potatoes and beetroot are tender. Serve with dollops of soured cream and plenty of chopped parsley.

tip Instead of leftover pork belly (page 51), you can use 400g sliced pork tenderloin quick-fried in a little oil at the start of the recipe.

Who says that a burger has to be made of mince? The tangy apples are the perfect foil for the leftover roast pork. Add a lick of yogurt or soured cream for an extra something.

1 TABLESPOON OLIVE OIL

1 RED ONION, FINELY SLICED

2 APPLES, SUCH AS COX, PEELED,
    CORED AND CUT INTO WEDGES

1 TEASPOON SMOKED SWEET PAPRIKA

2 TEASPOONS SOFT LIGHT BROWN
    SUGAR

2 TABLESPOONS KETCHUP

1 TABLESPOON WORCESTERSHIRE
    SAUCE

400G LEFTOVER SLOW-ROAST JUNIPER
    + FENNEL SEED PORK BELLY
    (PAGE 51), SHREDDED

BUNS OR BREAD, TO SERVE

SHREDDED PORK + APPLE BUNS

1. Heat the oil in a pan over a medium heat and fry the onion for 10 minutes until soft.

2. Add the apples and fry for 5 minutes before adding the remaining ingredients and a splash of water. Cook for 10 minutes until the pork is heated through and sticky then spoon into buns and serve.

tip If you haven't cooked the Slow-roast Juniper + Fennel Seed Pork Belly (page 51), you can make these into pork sloppy joes instead. Add 300g pork mince to the pan with the onion and fry until brown before adding the remaining ingredients. Spoon the pork mince into soft buns and serve with salad.

A pan full of golden, sizzling pork chops is a wonderful sight. The key to a fabulous chop is to not overcook it – it should be juicy and tender and almost a little pink in the middle before you eat it.

PAN-ROASTED PORK CHOPS WITH APPLES + ONIONS

SERVES **4**, PLUS LEFTOVERS
10 MINUTES TO MAKE
30 MINUTES TO COOK

4 LARGE OUTDOOR-REARED PORK
  CHOPS
1 TABLESPOON OLIVE OIL, PLUS EXTRA
  FOR BRUSHING
SEA SALT AND FRESHLY GROUND BLACK
  PEPPER
A HANDFUL OF SAGE LEAVES
2 ONIONS, FINELY SLICED
2-3 APPLES, PEELED AND CUT INTO
  WEDGES
100ML CHICKEN STOCK (PAGE 19)

1. Preheat the oven to 200°C/fan 180°C/gas 6. Brush the pork with the oil and season well. Heat an ovenproof frying or saute pan over a high heat and seal the pork on both sides until browned. Set aside.

2. Heat the oil in the pan and add the sage, onions and apples and fry for 5 minutes until they start to colour. Put the pork chops on top, splash in the stock and transfer to the oven and cook for 15-20 minutes until the pork is cooked and the apples and onions are sticky and tender.

3. Leave the pork to rest for 10 minutes then slice the meat from the bones, keeping the bones, and serve with the roasted apples and onions.

tip Although this recipe is for 4 pork chops, you will find that by slicing the meat from the bones you will have more than enough for the main recipe and for leftovers (see pages 58 and 59).

ENOUGH LEFT OVER FOR:
SPICED PORK WITH HARISSA CHICKPEAS (PAGE 58)
RAINBOW SALAD (PAGE 59) »——→

There are a lot of fantasic chilli pastes from around the world, from the trendy and exciting sriracha and gochujang to the good old favourite Tabasco, but harissa is one of the best. It is so handy to have a jar in the fridge to pep up leftovers. I prefer rose harissa as it has a slightly more delicate flavour.

SPICED PORK WITH HARISSA CHICKPEAS

SERVES 4
10 MINUTES TO MAKE
15 MINUTES TO COOK

1 TABLESPOON OLIVE OIL

1 ONION, FINELY SLICED

2 GARLIC CLOVES, CRUSHED

JUICE OF 1 LEMON

1 RED ONION, FINELY SLICED

SEA SALT AND FRESHLY GROUND BLACK
    PEPPER

300 LEFTOVER PAN-ROASTED
    PORK CHOPS (PAGE 55)

1 TABLESPOON ROSE HARISSA

2 X 400G CANS OF CHICKPEAS,
    DRAINED AND RINSED

SPLASH OF CHICKEN STOCK (PAGE 19)
    OR WATER

A HANDFUL OF CHOPPED FLAT-LEAF
    PARSLEY OR CORIANDER, TO FINISH

YOGURT, TO DOLLOP

1. Heat the oil in a pan and gently fry the onion for 10 minutes. Add the garlic and fry for 30 seconds. Squeeze half the lemon juice over the red onion with some seasoning and set aside to soften.

2. Meanwhile, remove any meat from the bones of the pork chops. Add this and the other pork to the pan with the harissa and toss to coat. Add the chickpeas and stock or water, season and simmer for 5–10 minutes.

3. Add the remaining lemon juice to the chickpeas. Serve the chickpeas with the red onion, scattered with herbs and splodged with yogurt.

tip If you haven't cooked the Pan-roasted Pork Chops (page 55), slice 300g pork steaks or tenderloin and fry in a little oil until just cooked. Add a splash of cider or stock and a few sage leaves and simmer for a couple of minutes.

The idea behind a rainbow salad is that anything goes, pack in as many different coloured vegetables as you can. This can be a winter or a summer salad, and is just as delicious with kale and beetroot as it is with sliced asparagus, peas and beans.

SERVES **4**
15 MINUTES TO MAKE
5 MINUTES TO COOK

2 BEETROOT, PEELED

2 CARROTS, PEELED

1 CUCUMBER

½ RED OR WHITE CABBAGE

A FEW SPRING ONIONS

300G LEFTOVER PAN-ROASTED PORK CHOPS (PAGE 55)

1 TEASPOON OLIVE OIL

DRIZZLE OF HONEY

A HANDFUL OF MIXED NUTS AND SEEDS, SUCH AS SUNFLOWER SEEDS, HAZELNUTS OR ALMONDS

FOR THE DRESSING

JUICE OF ½ LEMON

SEA SALT AND FRESHLY GROUND BLACK PEPPER

2 TEASPOONS DIJON MUSTARD

PINCH OF CASTER SUGAR

3 TABLESPOONS EXTRA VIRGIN OLIVE OIL

1 TABLESPOON WALNUT OIL

RAINBOW SALAD

1. Finely slice your veggies however you like, use a potato peeler to make ribbons, slice into batons, grate, or finely slice, whatever takes your fancy. Toss them all together in a bowl.

2. Remove any meat from the pork chop bones and add to any leftover slices of pork. Heat the oil in a pan over a medium heat and add the pork and honey and toss together until warm then add to the salad bowl with the nuts and seeds.

3. To make the dressing, whisk the lemon juice with the sea salt, pepper and sugar, then gradually whisk in the mustard then the oils. Pour over the salad and toss together and serve.

tip This really is an utterly versatile salad so if you don't have leftover pork chops (page 55), you could slice and fry pork tenderloin, pork escalope or even pork mince to make this recipe.

Pork mince often gets overlooked in favour of lamb or beef but to me it is one of the most versatile meats and is especially great with Asian flavours, as it is perfect for quick cooking.

LEMONGRASS + GINGER PORK

SERVES **4**, PLUS LEFTOVERS
10 MINUTES TO MAKE
15 MINUTES TO COOK

2 TABLESPOONS OLIVE OIL

2 STICKS LEMONGRASS, PEELED AND
   CENTRES FINELY SLICED

3CM PIECE OF FRESH GINGER,
   PEELED AND CUT INTO MATCHSTICKS

2 GARLIC CLOVES, FINELY SLICED

2 RED CHILLIES, FINELY SLICED

1 BUNCH SPRING ONIONS, FINELY
   SLICED

800G PORK MINCE

200G GREENS, SUCH AS SPROUT TOPS,
   SAVOY CABBAGE OR COLLARD
   GREENS

2 TABLESPOONS DARK OR LIGHT SOY
   SAUCE

300G RICE NOODLES

1 TABLESPOON SESAME OIL

SEA SALT AND FRESHLY GROUND BLACK
   PEPPER

LIME JUICE, TO TASTE

CHOPPED CORIANDER, TO SERVE

1. Heat the oil in a wok or pan over a high heat and fry the lemongrass, ginger, garlic and chillies and half the spring onions for 30 seconds. Add the pork mince and fry for 5 minutes until browned all over. Add the greens and soy sauce and a splash of water and cook for 10 minutes, stirring constantly.

2. To cook the noodles, put in a bowl, pour over a kettle full of boiling water and leave to stand for 10 minutes until cooked. Drain and toss with the sesame oil.

3. Season the pork, add the lime juice and coriander to taste and serve with the noodles scattered with the remaining spring onions.

ENOUGH LEFT OVER FOR:
SZECHUAN PORK + AUBERGINE BITES (PAGE 62)
PORK + PRAWN STEAMED DUMPLINGS (PAGE 64) ⟫⟶

Szechuan cooking is one of my favourites; the mouth-tingling, slightly numbing effect that nibbling on a Szechaun peppercorn has is a little addictive. Make sure that you really soften the aubergine properly for this recipe as it will bind the pork with its soft, silky texture.

MAKES **12**
20 MINUTES TO MAKE
20 MINUTES TO COOK

SZECHUAN PORK + AUBERGINE BITES

OLIVE OIL, TO FRY

1 AUBERGINE, CUT INTO 1CM PIECES

2 TEASPOONS SZECHUAN PEPPERCORNS

1 TEASPOON CHINESE FIVE SPICE

300G LEFTOVER LEMONGRASS + GINGER PORK (PAGE 61)

PLAIN FLOUR, TO DUST

2 X 375G PACKS READY-ROLLED ALL-BUTTER PUFF PASTRY

1 FREE-RANGE EGG, BEATEN

SESAME SEEDS, TO SPRINKLE

1. Heat the oil in a pan over a medium heat and fry the aubergine for 10–15 minutes until very tender. Add the spices and leftover pork and toss to combine. Set aside to cool.

2. Preheat the oven to 200°C/fan 180°C/gas mark 6. Roll out each block of pastry onto a lightly floured surface to a 30 x 20cm rectangle. Cut 6 x 10cm squares from each block. Fill each of the squares with the pork mix then bring the edges up to meet in the middle and pinch to seal. Place on a baking tray.

3. Brush all over with the beaten egg and sprinkle with sesame seeds. Bake for 15–20 minutes until puffed and golden.

tip You can easily make this recipe if you haven't made the Lemongrass + Ginger Pork on page 61, just fry 300g pork mince and add a good splash of any soy sauce.

Buy a few packets of dumpling or wonton wrappers from a Chinese supermarket and chuck them in the freezer for moments like this. It is worth buying a proper bamboo steamer if you like dumplings, they are pretty inexpensive and ideal for dumplings as the steam penetrates more evenly than in a metal steamer.

MAKES **24–28**
30 MINUTES TO MAKE
5–10 MINUTES TO COOK

200G LEFTOVER LEMONGRASS +
  GINGER PORK (PAGE 61)
200G RAW KING PRAWNS, SHELLED
  AND MINCED WITH A SHARP KNIFE
2 TEASPOONS GRATED FRESH GINGER
3 SPRING ONIONS, FINELY CHOPPED
1 TABLESPOON DARK OR LIGHT SOY
  SAUCE
1 TABLESPOON SESAME OIL
30 DUMPLING WRAPPERS

FOR THE SAUCE
1 SMALL GREEN FINGER CHILLI,
  CHOPPED (DESEEDED IF YOU LIKE)
3 TABLESPOONS RICE WINE VINEGAR
1 TABLESPOON MIRIN
3 TABLESPOONS DARK OR LIGHT SOY
  SAUCE

PORK + PRAWN STEAMED DUMPLINGS

1. Mix all the ingredients except the wrappers together in a large bowl. Lay the wrappers flat and put a dollop of the mix in the middle of each one. Brush the edges with water and bring up the sides and squidge together with your fingers to form a sort of parcel. Place in a steamer and steam for 5–7 minutes until the prawns are pink and the wrappers are translucent.

2. Mix together the sauce ingredients in a small bowl and serve with the dumplings. If you don't have the time or ingredients to make the sauce you can serve with sweet chilli sauce instead.

tip If you haven't cooked the Lemongrass + Ginger Pork on page 61, dry-fry 300g pork mince then add a splash of any soy sauce and cool.

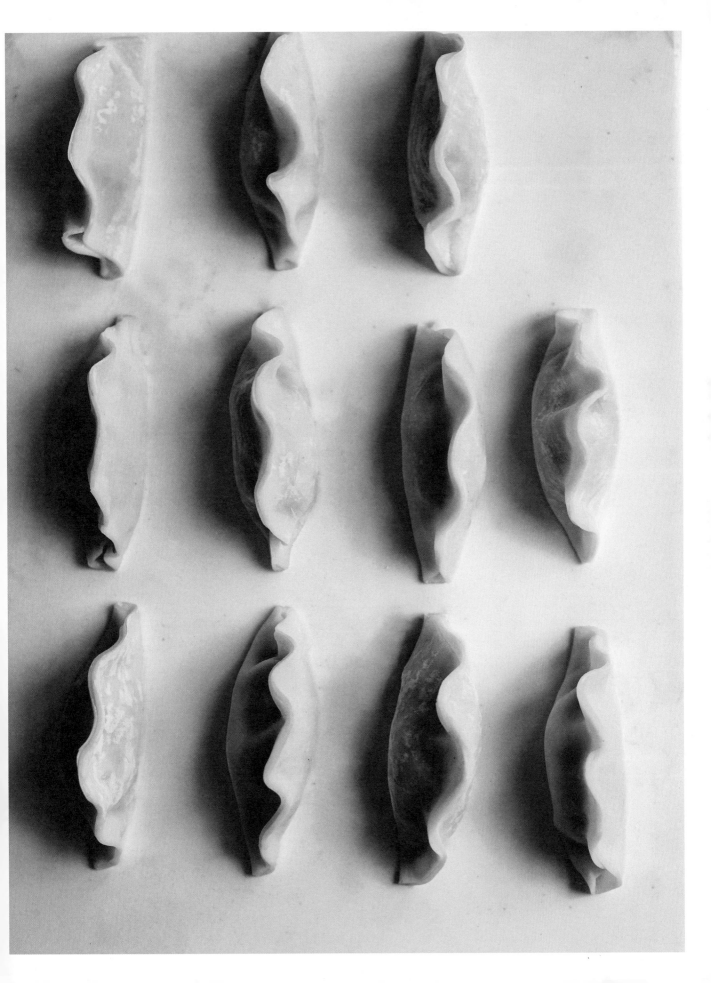

Until you have tried it, it's hard to explain the joy of a big steaming bowl of Hainan chicken. This is one of those dishes that puts the world to rights no matter what kind of day you are having. This is an homage to my dear friend Dhruv Baker who introduced me to this amazing dish. I've slightly simplified my version but I don't think he will mind me saying it is as perfectly delicious.

SERVES **4**, PLUS LEFTOVERS
25 MINUTES TO MAKE
30 MINUTES TO COOK

CHICKEN HAINAN

200ML OLIVE OIL

2 LARGE ONIONS, FINELY SLICED

SEA SALT

8 CHICKEN THIGH FILLETS

500ML FRESH CHICKEN STOCK
   (PAGE 19)

3CM PIECE OF FRESH GINGER, PEELED
   AND CUT INTO MATCHSTICKS

100G BUNCH FRESH CORIANDER

2 STAR ANISE

1 BUNCH SPRING ONIONS, SLICED INTO
   3CM PIECES

1 TABLESPOON TOASTED SESAME OIL

250G SPRING GREENS, SAVOY CABBAGE,
   CHARD, KALE OR BROCCOLI,
   SHREDDED

300G BASMATI RICE

4 TABLESPOONS DARK OR LIGHT SOY
   SAUCE

4 TABLESPOONS RICE WINE OR MALT
   VINEGAR

2 GREEN FINGER CHILLIES, SLICED

½ CUCUMBER, DESEEDED AND SLICED
   INTO QUARTER MOONS

150G CHERRY TOMATOES, QUARTERED

1. Heat the oil in a frying pan and very gently fry the onions with a pinch of salt until they are golden brown and crisp. Remove with a slotted spoon and drain on kitchen paper.

2. Put the chicken in a pan and pour over the stock and 750ml water, add the ginger, the stalks of the coriander, the star anise and half the spring onions. Bring to the boil and simmer for 15-20 minutes until the chicken is cooked. Scoop out the chicken and cut into small pieces. Put about half into a bowl for a leftover recipe such as Soul Soup (page 68) or Coconut + Chilli Chicken Pots (page 69), toss the remainder in the sesame oil and return to the pan with the greens and simmer until just tender.

3. Meanwhile, cook the rice in boiling salted water for 10 minutes until tender. Drain and set aside.

4. Mix the soy with the vinegar and the chillies. Spoon the rice into 4 bowls. Use a slotted spoon to scoop the chicken and bits into the bowls and then pour over a ladleful of soup. Drizzle with the soy mixture and scatter with the cucumber, cherry tomatoes and crispy onions. Garnish with the remaining spring onions and coriander.

tip A great way to make this recipe if you have a bit more time is to simmer a whole chicken in the fragrant stock for an hour until it is cooked. This not only adds bags of extra flavour but gives you lots more leftover chook to make other recipes with.

ENOUGH LEFT OVER FOR:
SOUL SOUP (PAGE 68)
COCONUT + CHILLI CHICKEN POTS (PAGE 69) »——→

What is it about chicken soup that nourishes the soul? Whether it does have true medicinal properties or if it is just because it tastes so good, it is the perfect pick-me-up for when you are feeling run-down. The intense broth from the Hainan provides the perfect platform on which to build the ultimate leftovers soup.

SERVES **2**
5 MINUTES TO MAKE
10 MINUTES TO COOK

SOUL SOUP

1 TABLESPOON OLIVE OIL

1 ONION, FINELY SLICED

2 STICKS CELERY, FINELY SLICED

500ML LEFTOVER CHICKEN HAINAN BROTH (PAGE 67)

100G ANGEL HAIR PASTA, BROKEN INTO SMALL BITS

150G SPRING GREENS, SAVOY OR POINTY CABBAGE, CHARD, KALE OR BROCCOLI, SHREDDED

A SMALL HANDFUL OF CHOPPED DILL

1. Heat the oil in a saucepan and gently fry the onion and celery for 10 minutes until softened. Add the broth and 200ml water and bring to the boil then add the pasta and greens. Simmer until the pasta is tender (just a couple of minutes) then stir in the dill and serve. If you have any chicken left over from your Hainan, you can add that to the soup at the end too.

tip If you haven't cooked the Chicken Hainan (page 67), then use good-quality fresh chicken stock (page 19) and simmer with a 2cm piece of chopped fresh ginger and a couple of star anise.

Pot pies are a great favourite of mine, just about anything tastes good under a crust of golden crispy pastry. This one is packed full of spice and flavour with a rich hit of coconut. Shop-bought puff is a great standby to have in your freezer to transform your leftovers.

SERVES **4**
15 MINUTES TO MAKE
30 MINUTES TO COOK

1 TABLESPOON OLIVE OIL

1 BUNCH SPRING ONIONS, FINELY CHOPPED

1 GARLIC CLOVE, FINELY SLICED

1 GREEN FINGER CHILLI, OR OTHER CHILLI, FINELY CHOPPED

250ML LEFTOVER HAINAN BROTH (PAGE 67)

1 TEASPOON CORNFLOUR

400ML CAN OF COCONUT MILK

250G SPRING GREENS, SAVOY OR POINTY CABBAGE, CHARD, KALE OR BROCCOLI, SHREDDED

4 LEFTOVER COOKED CHICKEN THIGHS (PAGE 67), CHOPPED

SEA SALT AND FRESHLY GROUND BLACK PEPPER

375G PACK READY-ROLLED ALL-BUTTER PUFF PASTRY

1 FREE-RANGE EGG, BEATEN

COCONUT + CHILLI CHICKEN POTS

1. Heat the oil in a pan and gently fry the spring onions for a few minutes then add the garlic and chilli and fry for a further minute. Mix a little broth with the cornflour until smooth then add to the plan with the remaining broth. Add the coconut milk, greens and chicken and season. Remove from the heat and divide between 4 x 300ml pots.

2. Preheat the oven to 200°C/fan 180°C/gas 6. Unroll the pastry and cut out lids to fit your pots. Use the leftover pastry trimmings to fix the lids to the rims of your pots then brush all over with beaten egg and bake for 20 minutes until puffed and golden.

tip If you haven't made the Chicken Hainan (page 67), then use 4 chopped chicken thigh fillets and simmer in 250ml chicken stock with a star anise until cooked then continue with the recipe as above.

BAKED SALMON WITH FENNEL + LEMON
FISHCAKES
SALMON + KALE OMELETTE

GIN + HERB-CURED SALMON
CURED SALMON KEDGEREE
PINK + GREEN TART

PAN-FRIED MACKEREL WITH CAPERS + BROWN BUTTER
MACKEREL, CHIVE, LEEK + CRÈME FRAÎCHE POTS
MACKEREL + ROCKET TAGLIATELLE

ROAST COD WITH HARISSA CHICKPEAS + CAULIFLOWER
CRISPY COD PATTIES
TABBOULEH SALAD

DRESSED CRAB
FRIED CRAB BITES
CRAB PASTA

GARLIC + TOMATO PRAWNS
PRAWN COCKTAIL
PRAWN BISQUE

HERB-CRUSTED BAKED COD
SUMMER SOUP
HERBY COD GRATINÉ

SEA

Cooking a whole fish or a large side is a wonderful way to both impress your friends and family and to ensure you have plenty of leftovers for the next day. In season, sea trout is a wonderful alternative to the usual salmon.

BAKED SALMON WITH FENNEL + LEMON

SERVES **4–6**, PLUS LEFTOVERS
10 MINUTES TO MAKE
25 MINUTES TO COOK

2 BULBS FENNEL, FINELY SLICED

2 LEMONS

1 SIDE SALMON, WEIGHING
   ABOUT 750G

SEA SALT AND FRESHLY GROUND BLACK
   PEPPER

1 SMALL BUNCH OF DILL

GOOD KNOB OF UNSALTED BUTTER

150ML WHITE WINE OR VERMOUTH

1. Preheat the oven to 180°C/fan 160°C/gas 4. Line a roasting tin with foil and scatter the fennel into it. Slice one of the lemons and scatter the slices into the tin then put the fish, skin-side down, on top. Season and scatter with the dill. Dot all over with the butter.

2. Pour the wine around the outside of the fish and add the juice of the other lemon. Bring the foil up and over and scrunch to form a parcel. Roast for 20–25 minutes until it is just opaque and you can flake it gently with a fork or the tip of a knife.

ENOUGH LEFT OVER FOR:
FISHCAKES (PAGE 74)
SALMON + KALE OMELETTE (PAGE 76) »——→

There are two types of fishcakes, classic potato ones and the more adventurous Thai-style ones. I had a hard time deciding between them but in the end the classic fishcake won. The key to a really good fishcake is the potato, it needs to be really dry and fluffy or your fishcake will become heavy and soggy.

SERVES **4**
25 MINUTES TO MAKE
45 MINUTES TO COOK

FISHCAKES

750G MEDIUM FLOURY POTATOES,
SUCH AS KING EDWARD OR MARIS
PIPER, LEFT WHOLE AND UNPEELED
GOOD KNOB OF UNSALTED BUTTER
SPLASH OF MILK
300G LEFTOVER BAKED SALMON WITH
FENNEL + LEMON (PAGE 73)
A HANDFUL OF CHOPPED SOFT HERBS,
SUCH AS PARSLEY, TARRAGON, DILL
OR CHIVES
2 TABLESPOONS CHOPPED
CORNICHONS, GHERKINS, CAPERS OR
CAPERBERRIES
SEA SALT AND FRESHLY GROUND BLACK
PEPPER
PLAIN FLOUR, TO DUST
2 FREE-RANGE EGGS, BEATEN
100G FRESH OR DRIED BREADCRUMBS
SUNFLOWER OIL, TO FRY

1. Put the potatoes into a pan of cold, salted water, bring to the boil and cook for 30–45 minutes or until they are tender when pierced. Drain and leave until cold enough to handle.

2. Peel off the skins and mash or rice the potatoes and mix with the butter and milk. Stir in the fish, herbs and pickles, season and shape into 8 patties. Chill for 30 minutes.

3. Dust the patties with plain flour then dip in the beaten egg and then the breadcrumbs. Heat a good layer of oil in a non-stick frying pan over a medium-high heat and fry for 5 minutes then turn over and fry until golden on both sides and hot in the centre.

tip Use flaked hot-smoked salmon or pan-fry a small piece or salmon or other fish to use in this recipe if you haven't cooked the Baked Salmon with Fennel + Lemon on page 73.

Kale is the darling of the vegetable world at the moment, and for good reason, as it is, apart from being packed with good-for-you vitamins, really delicious. Salmon is a robust fish and is a great match for this iron-rich brassica.

SERVES **2**
5 MINUTES TO MAKE
5 MINUTES TO COOK

150G CURLY KALE OR CAVOLO NERO

6 FREE-RANGE EGGS

SEA SALT AND FRESHLY GROUND BLACK
    PEPPER

300G LEFTOVER BAKED SALMON WITH
    FENNEL + LEMON (PAGE 73)

A HANDFUL OF CHOPPED SOFT
    HERBS, SUCH AS BASIL, DILL,
    PARSLEY, TARRAGON

DRIZZLE OF OLIVE OIL

FEW DOLLOPS CREAM CHEESE OR A
    LITTLE GRATED PARMESAN OR BOTH

SALMON + KALE OMELETTE

1. Plunge the kale or cavolo nero into boiling water and cook for 2–3 minutes. Drain and cool under running water then finely chop.

2. Beat the eggs in a bowl with plenty of seasoning. Add the salmon, herbs and kale or cavolo nero. Mix well.

3. Heat a non-stick frying pan with a little oil over a medium–high heat and when hot, pour in half the egg mixture. Cook, stirring a little, for 2–3 minutes until almost set, add dollop of cream cheese and a scatter of Parmesan then fold in half and slide onto a plate. Repeat with the other half of the mixture and serve.

tip Use flaked hot-smoked salmon if you don't have any leftover Baked Salmon (page 73).

Why is it that curing your own salmon seems to be something only ever done for big celebrations such as Christmas or Easter? It makes for a fantastic supper standby as well as being on hand for breakfasts, lunches and canapés.

GIN + HERB-CURED SALMON

SERVES **4–6**, PLUS LEFTOVERS
20 MINUTES TO MAKE
3–4 DAYS TO CURE

1.5KG WHOLE SALMON, FILLETED, SKIN ON
100ML GIN
75G DEMERARA SUGAR
50G SEA SALT
GOOD GRINDING OF BLACK PEPPER
25G DILL, FINELY CHOPPED
2 TABLESPOONS JUNIPER BERRIES
SLICES OF WHITE OR BROWN BREAD, SOFTENED UNSALTED BUTTER AND LEMON WEDGES, TO SERVE

1. Remove any bones from the salmon. Place one half, skin-side down, on a large piece of foil topped with a large piece of clingfilm. Rub with half the gin then mix the sugar, salt, pepper, herbs and juniper together and press over the salmon fillet.

2. Drizzle with a little more gin then place the other fillet, skin-side up, on top. Sprinkle with the remaining gin then fold the clingfilm up and over and tightly seal the salmon. Then bring the foil up and tightly seal that around the fish.

3. Place on a wire rack in a roasting tin or on a platter and then put a chopping board on top and weigh it down with some cans. Put the whole lot in the fridge and leave for 3–4 days, turning from time to time.

4. When ready, remove the wrappings and gently scrape away the salty herb mix with your finger and wipe with damp kitchen paper. Use a very sharp knife to cut thin slices of salmon away from the skin. Butter the slices of white or brown bread and serve with the cured salmon and lemon wedges. The salmon will keep in the fridge for at least a week.

ENOUGH LEFT OVER FOR:
CURED SALMON KEDGEREE (PAGE 80)
PINK + GREEN TART (PAGE 82) ⟶

My mother used to make kedgeree for us all the time, both the classic smoked haddock version and a cheat's version with canned tuna, which is one of my store cupboard suppers to this day. So the idea of using cured salmon in kedgeree was just the next step in the journey and it turns out it is gloriously delicious!

SERVES **4**
10 MINUTES TO MAKE
15 MINUTES TO COOK

3 FREE-RANGE EGGS

1 TABLESPOON OLIVE OIL

GOOD KNOB OF UNSALTED BUTTER

1 LARGE ONION, FINELY SLICED

1 TEASPOON GROUND TURMERIC

350G BASMATI RICE

300G LEFTOVER GIN + HERB-CURED
   SALMON (PAGE 79)

GOOD GLUG OF DOUBLE CREAM

A HANDFUL OF FLAT-LEAF PARSLEY,
   CHOPPED

SEA SALT AND FRESHLY GROUND BLACK
   PEPPER

CURED SALMON KEDGEREE

1. Put the eggs into cold water, bring to the boil and boil for 6 minutes. Drain and cool in cold water.

2. Meanwhile, heat the oil and butter in a pan and fry the onion for 10 minutes. Add the turmeric and stir for a minute.

3. Rinse the rice and then cook in a saucepan of boiling, salted water for 10–12 minutes until tender. Drain and add to the onion pan and toss to coat in the buttery yellowness. Add the salmon, cream and parsley and season well. Peel and halve the eggs and serve on top of scoops of the kedgeree.

tip If you don't have the Gin + Herb-cured Salmon (page 79), you can use smoked salmon instead or try flaked hot-smoked salmon or even good-quality tinned tuna.

Pink for salmon, green for whatever greeny veg you might have in your fridge, it really is that simple. I love making my own pastry, and find that I always have the ingredients to hand but a ready-rolled shortcrust would work well here too.

PINK + GREEN TART

FOR THE PASTRY

200G PLAIN FLOUR, PLUS EXTRA
    TO DUST

PINCH OF SALT

150G CHILLED UNSALTED BUTTER,
    CUBED

FOR THE FILLING

1 TABLESPOON OLIVE OIL

1 BUNCH OF SPRING ONIONS, FINELY
    SLICED

200G LEFTOVER GIN + HERB-CURED
    SALMON (PAGE 79), SLICED

200G GREEN VEGETABLES, SUCH AS
    ASPARAGUS, GREENS, SPROUTING
    BROCCOLI, SLICED AND BLANCHED IF
    NECESSARY

300ML DOUBLE CREAM, CRÈME
    FRAÎCHE OR A MIX OF BOTH

2 FREE-RANGE EGGS, PLUS 1 FREE-
    RANGE YOLK

2 TEASPOONS DIJON MUSTARD

A HANDFUL OF CHOPPED SOFT HERBS,
    SUCH AS TARRAGON, DILL OR
    PARSLEY

SEA SALT AND FRESHLY GROUND BLACK
    PEPPER

1. To make the pastry, blend the flour and salt together in a bowl then rub the cubes of butter in with your fingers until the mixture resembles breadcrumbs. Add 1–2 tablespoons of cold water and bring the mixture together with the flat of a knife then with your hands. Knead briefly and shape into a disc. Wrap in clingfilm and chill for 15 minutes.

2. Meanwhile, heat the oil in a saucepan and fry the spring onions for 5 minutes until softened. Tip into a bowl and add the salmon and green vegetables.

3. In a jug whisk the cream or crème fraîche with the eggs, yolk, mustard and herbs. Season.

4. Roll out the pastry on a lightly floured surface to 20mm in thickness and use to line a 20–23cm square or round tart tin. Chill for 10 minutes.

5. Preheat the oven to 200°C/fan 180°C/gas 6. Line the tart case with foil or baking parchment and baking beans or rice. Blind bake for 12–15 minutes then remove the foil/paper and beans/rice and return to the oven for a further 5 minutes.

6. Scatter the tart with the salmon mixture and pour over the egg and cream mixture. Reduce the oven temperature to 160°C/fan 140°C/gas 3 and bake for 20–30 minutes until just set. Leave to cool for at least 10 minutes before serving warm or at room temperature.

tip Use thin slices of smoked salmon if you don't have the cured salmon leftovers from page 79.

Mackerel is at its best when it's spankingly fresh so if you can, get yours from a good fishmonger and ask them to butterfly them for you. The capers cut through the oily flavour of the fish. Serve this simply with crusty bread or boiled new potatoes.

PAN-FRIED MACKEREL WITH CAPERS + BROWN BUTTER

SERVES **4**, PLUS LEFTOVERS
5 MINUTES TO MAKE
10 MINUTES TO COOK

1 TABLESPOON OLIVE OIL

6 MACKEREL, BUTTERFLIED

80G UNSALTED BUTTER

ZEST AND JUICE OF 1 LEMON

3 TABLESPOONS SMALL CAPERS, DRAINED AND RINSED

A HANDFUL OF FLAT-LEAF PARSLEY, FINELY CHOPPED

CRUSTY BREAD OR BOILED NEW POTATOES, TO SERVE

1. Heat a layer of oil in a non-stick frying pan and fry the mackerel, skin-side down, one or two at a time, for 4–5 minutes until golden brown then flip over and cook for 1 minute until just cooked through. Remove from the pan and keep warm in a low oven (about 100°C/fan 80°C/gas ½) while you cook the remaining fish.

2. Add the butter to the pan and allow to foam and start to become brown and nutty. Stir in the lemon zest and juice, capers and parsley. Serve the mackerel with the capers and butter and crusty bread or boiled new potatoes.

tip It takes no extra time to cook two more mackerel and you will reap the rewards the next day.

ENOUGH LEFT OVER FOR:
MACKEREL, CHIVE, LEEK + CRÈME FRAÎCHE POTS (PAGE 86)
MACKEREL + ROCKET TAGLIATELLE (PAGE 86) ➤—→

A great little starter or a perfect nibble to serve with
a glass of bubbles.

SERVES 4–6
5 MINUTES TO MAKE
5 MINUTES TO COOK

MACKEREL, CHIVE, LEEK + CRÈME FRAÎCHE POTS

GOOD KNOB OF UNSALTED BUTTER

2 LEEKS, FINELY SLICED

200G LEFTOVER PAN-FRIED MACKEREL
   WITH CAPERS + BROWN BUTTER,
   FLAKED (PAGE 85)

1 BUNCH OF CHIVES, SNIPPED

150G CRÈME FRAÎCHE

ZEST OF 1 LEMON AND SQUEEZE OF
   JUICE

2 TEASPOONS CREAMED HORSERADISH

FINGERS OF TOAST, TO SERVE

1. Heat the butter in a saucepan and gently fry the leeks for
5–6 minutes until soft. Tip into a bowl and set aside to cool.
Once cooled, mix with the remaining ingredients. Season and
spoon into small ramekins or pots and serve with toast fingers.

tip If you don't have leftover mackerel from page 85, use 200g
hot-smoked mackerel and add 2 teaspoons of drained and rinsed
capers instead.

Pasta is probably most people's go-to store cupboard supper and
a little leftover mackerel is just the thing to toss through at the end.
Many Italians say never to serve Parmesan with fish but in pasta
I always find it really rather good.

SERVES 4
5 MINUTES TO MAKE
12 MINUTES TO COOK

MACKEREL + ROCKET TAGLIATELLE

350G TAGLIATELLE OR OTHER LONG
   PASTA

200G LEFTOVER PAN-FRIED MACKEREL
   WITH CAPERS + BROWN BUTTER
   (PAGE 85), FLAKED

GOOD KNOB OF UNSALTED BUTTER

SPLASH OF CREAM, CRÈME FRAÎCHE
   OR SOURED CREAM

100G ROCKET

FRESHLY GROUND BLACK PEPPER

PARMESAN SHAVINGS, TO SERVE

1. Cook the pasta in boiling, salted water according to the packet
instructions or until just cooked. Drain and return to the pan
with a splash of cooking liquid and add the mackerel, butter,
cream and rocket. Season with plenty of black pepper and serve
scattered with Parmesan shavings.

tip Use 200g flaked hot-smoked mackerel if you haven't
cooked the Pan-fried Mackerel with Capers + Brown Butter
(page 85).

Roasting cauliflower makes such a difference, instead of absorbing all the water from steaming, it soaks up flavour like a sponge. Any firm, meaty white fish would be great in this recipe, something like haddock or even monkfish is fantastic.

ROAST COD WITH HARISSA CHICKPEAS + CAULIFLOWER

SERVES 4, PLUS LEFTOVERS
5 MINUTES TO MAKE
45 MINUTES TO COOK

1 CAULIFLOWER, BROKEN INTO
   FLORETS
2 TABLESPOONS OLIVE OIL
2 TABLESPOONS ROSE HARISSA
400G CAN OF CHOPPED TOMATOES
SPLASH OF VEGETABLE STOCK OR
   WATER
400G CAN OF CHICKPEAS, DRAINED
   AND RINSED
800G CHUNKY COD FILLETS
1 TABLESPOON OLIVE OIL
FRESH CORIANDER, CHOPPED,
   TO SCATTER

1. Preheat the oven to 190°C/fan 170°C/gas 5. Put the cauliflower into a roasting tin and toss with the oil and harissa. Roast for 25–30 minutes, turning occasionally.

2. Stir in the tomatoes and stock or water. Mix in the chickpeas then place the cod on top, drizzle with oil and season. Roast for a further 10–12 minutes until the cod is just cooked. Scatter with coriander and serve.

ENOUGH LEFT OVER FOR:
CRISPY COD PATTIES (PAGE 89)
TABBOULEH SALAD (PAGE 89) ⟶

I can't resist a patty, if I read the word on a menu I am instantly hooked. Little fried delicate patties of deliciousness. These guys are a little fragile so let them fry for a good few minutes over a medium heat until they have a nice crust before you flip them.

MAKES **8**
10 MINUTES TO MAKE
10 MINUTES TO COOK

CRISPY COD PATTIES

300G LEFTOVER ROAST COD WITH
   HARISSA CHICKPEAS +
   CAULIFLOWER (PAGE 88)
400G CAN OF CHICKPEAS, DRAINED
   AND RINSED
2 BEETROOT, PEELED AND GRATED
1 FREE-RANGE EGG, BEATEN
ZEST AND JUICE OF 1 LEMON
SEA SALT AND FRESHLY GROUND
   BLACK PEPPER
SUNFLOWER OIL, TO FRY
PLAIN FLOUR, TO DUST
GREEK OR NATURAL YOGURT, TO SERVE

1. Mash up the leftover cod, chickpeas and cauliflower and the additional can of chickpeas with a fork to form a rough paste. Add the grated beetroot, egg, lemon zest and juice and season to taste. Shape into patties and chill for 30 minutes.

2. Heat a good layer of oil in a non-stick frying pan. Dust the patties in flour and fry for 3–4 minutes on each side until golden. Serve with yogurt.

The thing about tabbouleh is that it is more about the parsley than about the bulgar wheat, so don't be shy when adding it to the bowl.

SERVES **4** AS A LUNCH OR **6** AS A SIDE
10 MINUTES TO MAKE
15 MINUTES TO COOK

TABBOULEH SALAD

300G BULGAR WHEAT
550ML VEGETABLE STOCK OR WATER
1 CUCUMBER OR COURGETTE
A HANDFUL OF ROUGHLY CHOPPED
   SOFT HERBS, SUCH AS TARRAGON,
   DILL OR PARSLEY
ZEST AND JUICE OF 1 LEMON
A GOOD GLUG OF EXTRA VIRGIN OLIVE
   OIL
300G LEFTOVER ROAST COD WITH
   HARISSA CHICKPEAS +
   CAULIFLOWER (PAGE 88)
SEA SALT AND FRESHLY GROUND
   BLACK PEPPER

1. Put the bulgar wheat in a saucepan and cover with the stock or water. Bring to the boil then cover and set aside, off the heat, for 15 minutes until the liquid has absorbed.

2. Use a peeler to peel the cucumber or courgette into ribbons. Toss them with the bulgar wheat with the remaining ingredients. Season and serve.

tip Break 150g raw cauliflower into small florets or whizz into crumbs. Mix with a 400g can of chickpeas, drained and rinsed. Pan-fry a 150g cod fillet and flake up to toss through the salad at the end. Add a little dollop of harissa to the stock before pouring over the bulgar wheat.

A perfectly dressed crab is a thing of beauty. It is simple these days to buy them from good fishmongers, but for me, the process of cracking open a just-cooked crab, with all its sea-fresh juices, and picking out the hard-to-get white meat, somehow makes the end result all the sweeter. A prize for all the hard work.

SERVES 4, PLUS LEFTOVERS
1 HOUR TO MAKE, PLUS FREEZING
15 MINUTES TO COOK

DRESSED CRAB

4 LIVE LARGE BROWN CRABS,
   WEIGHING ABOUT 900G-1KG EACH
25G FRESH WHITE BREADCRUMBS
FEW DASHES OF TABASCO SAUCE
GOOD SQUEEZE OF LEMON JUICE
2-3 TABLESPOONS MAYONNAISE
PINCH OF GROUND MACE
TOAST, TO SERVE

1. Put the crabs in the freezer for 15 minutes. Bring a very large pan of water to the boil and drop in the crabs. Cover and boil for 15 minutes. Remove from the water and set aside to cool.

2. Twist the claws and legs off the bodies and set aside for now. Put each crab on its back. Hold the edges of the shell with your fingers and then use your thumbs to push on where the leg section joins the body and lever the body away from the leg.

3. Pull off the feathery soft dead man's fingers sticking out from the body. Scoop out the bony, gloopy bits from behind the eyes and discard.

4. Scrape out all the brown meat from the sides of the shell into a bowl and set aside. Use the back of a heavy knife or hammer to crack open the claws so that you can remove all of the juicy meat. Make sure you break open the knuckles and legs to get every last bit.

5. Cut the body section in half and use a skewer or lobster pick to pick out all the sweet white meat from the many compartments. Wash and dry the shells.

tips Choose crabs that feel heavy for their size. If your pan isn't very large, cook the crabs one or two at a time. Make sure the water comes fully to the boil before adding the next crab.

6. Mix the brown crabmeat with the breadcrumbs and Tabasco and spoon into the sides of each shell. Mix the white meat with a little lemon juice, some mayonnaise and mace and spoon into the centre of the shells. Serve with hot toast.

ENOUGH LEFT OVER FOR:
FRIED CRAB BITES (PAGE 92)
CRAB PASTA (PAGE 94) ⟫⟶

Naughty but nice, these golden fried nuggets of crab are really moreish with a little squidge of lemon. They brown in seconds in the oil so watch them like a hawk in case they go too dark.

MAKES **8–10**
15 MINUTES TO MAKE
5 MINUTES TO COOK

FRIED CRAB BITES

175G LEFTOVER DRESSED CRAB
  (PAGE 91)
100G RITZ BISCUITS, WATER BISCUITS
  OR SIMPLE CRACKERS, CRUSHED TO
  CRUMBS
FEW DROPS OF TABASCO SAUCE
2 TEASPOONS DIJON MUSTARD
SUNFLOWER OIL, FOR DEEP-FRYING
1 FREE-RANGE EGG, BEATEN
LEMON WEDGES, TO SERVE

1. Mix the crab with 2 teaspoons of crackers and the Tabasco and mustard. Shape into 8–10 walnut-sized balls and chill for 20 minutes.

2. Heat the oil in a small but deep pan until it reaches 180°C or a cube of bread browns in 30 seconds.

3. Dip each ball in the beaten egg and then into the remaining crushed crackers and fry for a minute or so until golden brown. Serve straight away with lemon wedges on the side.

tip Buy a medium dressed crab to make this recipe if you haven't dressed your own crab (page 91).

A freshly dressed crab is heaven but it is quite rich so I often find I have some left over and always think simple is best when it comes to such a delicious treat. Tossed through pasta with fresh herbs is about as good as a second helping of crab gets.

SERVES 4
5 MINUTES TO MAKE
12 MINUTES TO COOK

350G LINGUINE OR OTHER LONG PASTA
SEA SALT AND FRESHLY GROUND BLACK
  PEPPER
EXTRA VIRGIN OLIVE OIL, TO DRIZZLE
200G LEFTOVER DRESSED CRAB
  (PAGE 91)
A HANDFUL OF CHOPPED SOFT HERBS,
  SUCH AS PARSLEY, TARRAGON,
  CHIVES, DILL OR BASIL
GRATED PARMESAN, TO SERVE

CRAB PASTA

1. Cook the pasta in boiling, salted water accoridng to the packet instructions until just cooked and al dente. Return to the pan with a little of the cooking water and a good drizzle of extra virgin olive oil.

2. Toss through the crab and herbs and season with sea salt and plenty of freshly ground black pepper. Serve immediately with Parmesan grated over the top.

tip Use a mix of mostly white with a little brown crab if you didn't dress your own crab (page 91).

Served as a simple quick supper or as part of a tapas menu for friends these prawns are simply delicious. A cunning little trick is to buy raw prawns in their shells, that way, even if you have very few prawns left after scoffing you have the shells and heads to make a fabulous stock or soup.

GARLIC + TOMATO PRAWNS

SERVES **4**, PLUS LEFTOVERS
10 MINUTES TO MAKE
20 MINUTES TO COOK

2 TABLESPOONS OLIVE OIL
1 BANANA SHALLOT, FINELY CHOPPED
3 GARLIC CLOVES, FINELY SLICED
125ML DRY WHITE WINE
A SPRIG OF ROSEMARY
400G CAN OF CHERRY TOMATOES
700G SHELL-ON KING PRAWNS

1. Heat the oil in a pan and gently fry the shallot for 5 minutes then add the garlic and cook for 30 seconds. Add the wine, rosemary and tomatoes and bubble for 10–12 minutes then add the prawns and cook until they are pink. Season to taste and serve immediately. Keep the heads and shells for the Prawn Bisque on page 99.

ENOUGH LEFT OVER FOR:
PRAWN COCKTAIL (PAGE 98)
PRAWN BISQUE (PAGE 99) »——→

Now considered by many to be so retro that it is cool again, the humble prawn cocktail is always a winner. Using up the leftover Garlic + Tomato Prawns (page 95) adds a whole new dimension to the dish, which once tried you may never do any other way.

SERVES **4**

10 MINUTES TO MAKE

PRAWN COCKTAIL

150G GARLIC + TOMATO PRAWNS
- ABOUT 8-10 PRAWNS AND
4-5 TABLESPOONS SAUCE
(PAGE 95)
5 TABLESPOONS MAYONNAISE
A SQUIDGE OF TOMATO KETCHUP
DASH OF TABASCO SAUCE
DASH OF WORCESTERSHIRE SAUCE
SQUEEZE OF LEMON JUICE
TINY SPLASH OF SHERRY
SEA SALT AND FRESHLY GROUND BLACK
PEPPER
ANY GREEN SALAD BITS YOU HAVE,
SUCH AS LETTUCE, AVOCADO,
CUCUMBER
BREAD OR TOAST, TO SERVE

1. Remove any prawns from the sauce and roughly chop. Mix the sauce with the mayonnaise, tomato ketchup, Tabasco, Worcestershire sauce, lemon juice and sherry. Season to taste and stir in the chopped prawns.

2. Chop any salad bits you have and put onto small plates. Top with the prawn cocktail and serve with crusty bread or toast.

tip If you haven't made the Garlic + Tomato Prawns on page 95, you can make a more classic prawn cocktail. Mix 10 cooked prawns, chopped if king prawns, and mix with the remaining ingredients, adding a little more mayo and tomato sauce.

The word bisque makes this recipe sound way more difficult or flashy than it really is, it is just that to call it a soup would be to do it an injustice as it has such a fabulous depth of flavour and a silky smoothness from the prawn shells.

SERVES 4 AS A STARTER
15 MINUTES TO MAKE
50 MINUTES TO COOK

PRAWN BISQUE

2 TABLESPOONS OLIVE OIL

200-300G PRAWN SHELLS
  (SEE PAGE 95)

1 ONION, FINELY SLICED

1 CARROT, FINELY CHOPPED

2 TEASPOONS GREEN FENNEL SEEDS

150ML WHITE WINE

100-150G LEFTOVER GARLIC + TOMATO
  PRAWNS (PAGE 95)

400G CAN OF CHOPPED TOMATOES

700ML FISH OR VEGETABLE STOCK

GOOD SPLASH OF DOUBLE CREAM,
  CRÈME FRAÎCHE OR SOURED CREAM,
  TO SERVE

SEA SALT AND FRESHLY GROUND BLACK
  PEPPER

A HANDFUL OF SOFT HERBS, SUCH AS
  DILL, PARSLEY, TARRAGON OR
  FENNEL, FINELY CHOPPED, TO SERVE

1. Heat the oil in a pan and fry the shells from the prawns, onion, carrot and the fennel seeds for 10 minutes until the vegetables are lovely and soft. Add the wine and bubble for a minute.

2. Remove any leftover prawns from the sauce and set aside. Add the leftover sauce along with the chopped tomatoes and stock to the pan and simmer for 30 minutes.

3. Blitz the soup as finely as you can (shells and all) then pour through a sieve into a bowl, pressing out as much of the mixture through the sieve as you can.

4. Tip back into a clean pan and bring to the boil. Chop the prawns and add them to the pan with a glug of cream then whizz. Season to taste and serve with extra cream, crème fraiche or soured cream and any soft herbs you have knocking about.

tip Buy 300g shell-on prawns to use in this recipe if you haven't made the Garlic + Tomato Prawns (page 95).

Pressing a crust onto fish before baking is a great way to add loads of extra flavour and texture to the finished dish. It also protects the delicate fish from the heat of the oven so that the fish cooks perfectly.

HERB-CRUSTED BAKED COD

SERVES **4**, PLUS LEFTOVERS
15 MINUTES TO MAKE
15 MINUTES TO COOK

2 SIDES OF COD FILLET, WEIGHING
  ABOUT 350G EACH
SEA SALT AND FRESHLY GROUND BLACK
  PEPPER
150G FRESH WHITE BREADCRUMBS
1 GARLIC CLOVE, CRUSHED
ZEST OF 1 LEMON
A HANDFUL OF CHOPPED FLAT-LEAF
  PARSLEY
A HANDFUL OF CHOPPED SOFT HERBS,
  SUCH AS TARRAGON, CHIVES OR DILL
2 TABLESPOONS MAYONNAISE
1 TABLESPOON DIJON MUSTARD
2 TABLESPOONS CAPERS, CHOPPED
EXTRA VIRGIN OLIVE OIL, TO DRIZZLE

1. Preheat the oven to 200°C/fan 180°C/gas 6 and line a baking tray with baking paper.

2. Season the fish all over and put on the lined tray. Mix the remaining ingredients together, adding enough olive oil to bind and season. Press the mixture all over the fish and bake in the top of the oven for 12–15 minutes until the fish is just cooked and the crust is golden.

ENOUGH LEFT OVER FOR:
SUMMER SOUP (PAGE 102)
HERB COD GRATINÉ (PAGE 102) »——→

An English summer is full to bursting with amazing green tender vegetables and what better way to celebrate it than in the most simple broth with flakes of white fish and crispy crumbs.

SERVES **4** AS A STARTER
10 MINUTES TO MAKE
20 MINUTES TO COOK

SUMMER SOUP

1 TABLESPOON OLIVE OIL

1 LARGE ONION, FINELY SLICED

2 GARLIC CLOVES, CRUSHED

400G GREEN SUMMER VEGETABLES, SUCH AS FENNEL, ASPARAGUS, LEEKS OR PEAS, SLICED IF NECESSARY

150ML WHITE WINE

500ML VEGETABLE STOCK

SEA SALT AND FRESHLY GROUND BLACK PEPPER

300G LEFTOVER HERB-CRUSTED BAKED COD (PAGE 101)

1. Heat the oil in a pan and fry the onion for 10 minutes until softened. Add the garlic and the green vegetables and stir well for 30 seconds. Add the wine and bubble for a couple of minutes then add the stock. Season and simmer for 5–10 minutes.

2. Flake the fish, keeping the crust aside, and add to the soup. Once hot, serve in deep bowls with a scattering of the crust over the top.

Here a simple white sauce and cheesy crust transforms leftover fish into a supper to chase away the rainy day blues.

SERVES **2**
15 MINUTES TO MAKE
15 MINUTES TO COOK

HERBY COD GRATINÉ

20G UNSALTED BUTTER

20G PLAIN FLOUR

250ML WHOLE MILK

2 TEASPOONS DIJON MUSTARD

SEA SALT AND FRESHLY GROUND BLACK PEPPER

300G GREEN VEGETABLES, SUCH AS LEEKS, PEAS, SPROUTS

200G LEFTOVER HERB-CRUSTED BAKED COD (PAGE 101)

A HANDFUL OF SOFT HERBS, SUCH AS TARRAGON, PARSLEY, CHIVES OR DILL

25G GRATED CHEESE, SUCH AS CHEDDAR, GRUYÈRE OR PARMESAN

1. Preheat the oven to 200°C/fan 180°C/gas 6. Melt the butter in a pan, add the flour and cook for 2–3 minutes then gradually add the milk, stirring until you have a thick creamy sauce. Add the mustard and season well.

2. Blanch the green vegetables and add to the white sauce. Remove the crust and set aside. Flake the fish into the sauce, chop the herbs and add them too and stir together.

3. Spoon into an ovenproof dish. Break the crust up into small pieces and scatter over the top along with the cheese. Bake for 10–12 minutes until bubbling and hot.

tip If don't have the leftover cod (page 101), simply pan-fry 300g cod or white fish fillet until just cooked. Flake and mix with the white sauce. Scatter over a handful of breadcrumbs.

CAULIFLOWER CHEESE
CAULIFLOWER CHEESE SOUP
CAULIFLOWER CHEESE, CUMIN + TURMERIC FRITTERS

SPROUTING BROCCOLI, SHERRY + ALMONDS
BAKED EGGS WITH SPROUTING BROCCOLI
GIANT COUSCOUS + SPROUTING BROCCOLI

BEST EVER MASHED POTATO
MASHED POTATO PASTRY
POTATO + BLUE CHEESE CROQUETTES

BAKED BEETROOT WITH SOURED CREAM + HERBS
BEETROOT PILAF
BEETROOT + FETA CAKE

SCANDI POTATO SALAD
POTATO SALAD ROASTIES
FRITTATA

BRAISED RED CABBAGE
RED CABBAGE CHUTNEY
MIXED PICKLED BRASSICA SLAW

ROAST AUBERGINE + TOMATOES
PASTA BAKE WITH AUBERGINE + TOMATOES
AUBERGINE + TOMATO MINI CALZONES

ROOT VEGETABLE GRATIN
GRATIN HASH WITH POACHED EGGS
SAVOURY GRATIN MUFFINS

BEST EVER TOMATO SAUCE
VEGGIE RISSOLES IN TOMATO SAUCE
POTATO + HALLOUMI IN SPICED TOMATO SAUCE

SPRING VEGETABLE + RICOTTA SALAD
SALAD FRY-UP
GREEN DIP

BAKED SQUASH WITH CHILLI + ROSEMARY
SQUASH + PARMESAN SOUFFLÉ
SQUASH LASAGNE

GARDEN

This oozy, cheesy dish is a far cry from the dishcloth grey cauliflower with white sauce and barely a hint of cheese that you might remember from school. This is a dish to warm the cockles and wrap you in a blanket of contented wellbeing.

SERVES **4**, PLUS LEFTOVERS
20 MINUTES TO MAKE, PLUS INFUSING
20 MINUTES TO COOK

CAULIFLOWER CHEESE

75G UNSALTED BUTTER

50G PLAIN FLOUR

600ML WHOLE MILK

125G STRONG CHEDDAR OR A MIX OF
   ANY CHEESE YOU HAVE, PLUS EXTRA
   TO SPRINKLE

GOOD SPLASH OF DOUBLE CREAM

GOOD GRATING NUTMEG

PINCH OF MUSTARD POWDER

SEA SALT AND FRESHLY GROUND BLACK
   PEPPER

1 LARGE CAULIFLOWER, BROKEN INTO
   FLORETS

45G FRESH BREADCRUMBS

1. Melt the butter in a pan, add the flour and cook over a medium heat for a couple of minutes. Gradually add the milk, stirring, until you have a smooth thick sauce. Add the cheese, cream, nutmeg and mustard powder and season well.

2. Meanwhile, put the cauliflower in a steamer or pan of boiling water and steam or boil for 3–4 minutes until just tender. Drain and tip into the pan of sauce.

3. Heat the grill to medium–high. Tip the cauliflower into an ovenproof dish. Mix the breadcrumbs with some more cheese and sprinkle over the top. Grill for 4–5 minutes until golden and bubbling then serve.

ENOUGH LEFT OVER FOR:
CAULIFLOWER CHEESE SOUP (PAGE 108)
CAULIFLOWER CHEESE, CUMIN + TURMERIC
   FRITTERS (PAGE 110) »⟶

When I told my little sister that I was going to turn leftover cauliflower cheese into soup she looked at me as if I was a bit mad, but when she tasted the silky smooth velvet from the pan she was quickly convinced that this is the only way to use up any leftovers you might have.

SERVES **4**

5 MINUTES TO MAKE

20 MINUTES TO COOK

ABOUT 300G LEFTOVER CAULIFLOWER
   CHEESE (PAGE 107)
1 LARGE FLOURY POTATO, CUT INTO
   CHUNKS
700ML CHICKEN (PAGE 19)
   OR VEGETABLE STOCK
75ML DOUBLE CREAM
SEA SALT AND FRESHLY GROUND BLACK
   PEPPER

CAULIFLOWER CHEESE SOUP

1. Put the leftover cauliflower cheese, potato chunks and chicken stock into a pan and bring to the boil. Simmer for 20 minutes until the potato is tender.

2. Whizz the mixture with a stick blender until smooth then add the cream. Season to taste and serve.

tip If you haven't got any leftover Cauliflower Cheese (page 107), add 250–300g cauliflower to a pan and cook until tender. Add a good glug of double cream and 50–75g grated Cheddar or other cheese before whizzing.

Even if you only have a little scraping of leftovers then this is the recipe for you. Tiny cheese florets coated in a light, spiced crispy batter with plenty of scraps.

CAULIFLOWER CHEESE, CUMIN + TURMERIC FRITTERS

SERVES **4**

15 MINUTES TO MAKE

15 MINUTES TO COOK

200–300G LEFTOVER CAULIFLOWER
  CHEESE (PAGE 107)

SUNFLOWER OIL, TO FRY

50G PLAIN FLOUR

½ TEASPOON GROUND TURMERIC

1 TEASPOON CUMIN SEEDS

PINCH OF CHILLI FLAKES

1 FREE-RANGE EGG, BEATEN

75ML SPARKLING WATER

SEA SALT AND FRESHLY GROUND BLACK
  PEPPER

1. Separate the cauliflower florets into small pieces and chill until needed.

2. Heat the oil in a deep pan to 180°C or until a cube of bread browns in 30 seconds.

3. Mix the flour in a bowl with the spices, make a well in the centre, add the egg and start to mix, adding the sparkling water as you go. Mix until you have a smooth thick batter.

4. Dip the cauliflower cheese lumps into the batter then drop into the hot oil and fry for 1–2 minutes until golden, drain on kitchen paper, season and serve. You can fry any leftover batter, drizzled into the oil, as delicious scraps to go with the cauliflower too.

tip You can make these fritters with just plain blanched cauliflower florets, they won't have that lovely cheesy flavour but will be delicious all the same.

Broccoli doesn't need to be boring. The little trees are great absorbers of flavour and dressings. This would be a fantastic side dish for a roast or griddled chicken breast, but I think it would also make a fantastic simple lunch.

SPROUTING BROCCOLI, SHERRY + ALMONDS

SERVES **4** AS A SIDE, PLUS LEFTOVERS
5 MINUTES TO MAKE
15 MINUTES TO COOK

OLIVE OIL, TO FRY

3 BANANA SHALLOTS, FINELY SLICED

500G SPROUTING BROCCOLI

75ML SHERRY, SUCH AS OLOROSO OR
   MANZANILLA

SEA SALT AND FRESHLY GROUND BLACK
   PEPPER

50G BLANCHED ALMONDS, TOASTED

EXTRA VIRGIN OLIVE OIL, TO SERVE

1. Heat a good layer of oil in a non-stick frying pan and gently fry the shallots for 10 minutes until golden and crisp. Drain on kitchen paper.

2. Stand the broccoli in a deep pan with about 5cm of boiling water, cover and cook for 5-6 minutes until the stems are tender.

3. Meanwhile, heat 1 tablespoon of oil in a pan and add the cooked broccoli and splash in the sherry. Season and scatter with the almonds and crispy shallots. Drizzle with extra virgin olive oil to serve.

ENOUGH LEFT OVER FOR:
BAKED EGGS WITH SPROUTING BROCCOLI (PAGE 114)
GIANT COUSCOUS + SPROUTING BROCCOLI
   (PAGE 116) »⟶

It's those eggs again, helping to turn humble leftovers
into fabulous suppers!

SERVES 4
10 MINUTES TO MAKE
30 MINUTES TO COOK

1 TABLESPOON OLIVE OIL

1 LARGE ONION, FINELY SLICED

2 GARLIC CLOVES, CRUSHED

400G CAN OF CHOPPED TOMATOES

SEA SALT AND FRESHLY GROUND BLACK
  PEPPER

200G LEFTOVER SPROUTING BROCCOLI,
  SHERRY + ALMONDS (PAGE 113)

150G EXTRA BITS, SUCH AS CHOPPED
  BACON, CHORIZO, SALAMI OR
  SMOKED SALMON OR MACKEREL
  (OPTIONAL)

4 FREE-RANGE EGGS

BAKED EGGS WITH SPROUTING BROCCOLI

1. Preheat the oven to 180°C/fan 160°C/gas 4. Heat the oil in an
ovenproof non-stick frying pan and fry the onion for 10 minutes
until softened. Add the garlic and fry for 30 seconds then add the
tomatoes. Season and bubble for 10 minutes.

2. Chop the leftover broccoli into small pieces and add to the
pan. If you have any other bits to add then chuck them in (you
can crisp up any meaty bits first if you like).

3. Make four little wells in the mixture and crack an egg into each
one then pop into the oven and bake for 8–10 minutes until the
eggs are set but the yolks are still soft.

tip If you don't have any leftover broccoli then you can either
quickly make the Sprouting Broccoli, Sherry + Almonds (page 113)
or simply blanch 200g sprouting broccoli instead.

A great portable lunch or picnic dish, just toss it all together, pack up and go.

SERVES 4
5 MINUTES TO MAKE
5 MINUTES TO COOK

200G GIANT COUSCOUS OR
    COUSCOUS, BULGAR WHEAT OR A
    SMALL PASTA LIKE FREGOLA
500ML HOT VEGETABLE OR CHICKEN
    STOCK (PAGE 19)
200 LEFTOVER SPROUTING BROCCOLI,
    SHERRY + ALMONDS (PAGE 113)
SHAVINGS OF PARMESAN CHEESE
    OR ANY OTHER CHEESE, SUCH AS
    FETA, PECORINO, GOAT'S CHEESE OR
    BLUE CHEESE
JUICE OF 1 LEMON
SEA SALT AND FRESHLY GROUND BLACK
    PEPPER
PINCH OF DRIED CHILLI FLAKES
    (OPTIONAL)
EXTRA VIRGIN OLIVE OIL, TO DRIZZLE

GIANT COUSCOUS + SPROUTING BROCCOLI

1. Gently simmer the giant couscous in the hot stock for 5–6 minutes until tender. Roughly chop the broccoli and put into a bowl. Drain the couscous, toss in with the broccoli and add any bits of cheese you may have. Squeeze in the lemon juice to taste, add some seasoning and chilli flakes if you want, drizzle with olive oil and serve.

tip Without making the Sprouting Broccoli, Sherry + Almonds (page 113), simply blanch 200g sprouting or tenderstem broccoli before making this recipe. You can add a splash of sherry vinegar too if you have it.

It might seem basic to have a recipe for mashed potato but so many recipes don't do justice to this wonderful dish, which is the backbone of so many meals.

BEST EVER MASHED POTATO

SERVES **4**, PLUS LEFTOVERS
10 MINUTES TO MAKE
45–50 MINUTES TO COOK

1KG MEDIUM FLOURY POTATOES, SUCH
   AS KING EDWARD OR MARIS PIPER,
   LEFT WHOLE AND UNPEELED
SEA SALT AND FRESHLY GROUND BLACK
   PEPPER
50G UNSALTED BUTTER
GOOD SPLASH OF DOUBLE CREAM

1. Put the unpeeled potatoes into a pan of cold salted water. Bring to the boil and cook gently for 45–50 minutes until you can pierce them easily with a sharp knife or skewer.

2. Drain and leave until cool enough to handle then peel them and push them through a ricer. Add the butter and cream and stir together with plenty of seasoning.

tip Use as many even, medium-sized potatoes as you can so that they all cook at the same time to prevent some overcooking while others stay raw in the centre.

ENOUGH LEFT OVER FOR:
MASHED POTATO PASTRY (PAGE 118)
POTATO + BLUE CHEESE CROQUETTES (PAGE 119) »——→

Possibly the greatest pastry of all time. Rich and buttery, forgiving to work with, flaky and tender. This is my version of Josceline Dimbleby's original recipe from one of the best books of my childhood, *Marvellous Meals with Mince*!

MASHED POTATO PASTRY

MAKES ENOUGH FOR
1 LARGE PIE CRUST
15 MINUTES TO MAKE

200G SELF-RAISING FLOUR

SEA SALT

125G COLD UNSALTED BUTTER, CUBED

150G LEFTOVER BEST EVER MASHED
   POTATO (PAGE 117)

1 MEDIUM FREE-RANGE EGG YOLK

1. Put the flour in a bowl with a good pinch of salt. Add the butter and rub together with your fingertips until it resembles breadcrumbs. Add the mashed potato and egg yolk and mix with the blade of a knife. Then bring the mixture together with your hands and knead briefly. Shape the pastry into a disc, wrap in clingfilm and chill for at least 20 minutes before using.

2. Use as you would any other shortcrust pastry – for savoury dishes, pie crusts, tarts or tartlets and so on.

tip If you don't have any leftover Best Ever Mashed Potato (page 117), just cook 200g potatoes until tender and mash well. Leave to cool before using.

Croquettes, whether made with a potato or béchamel centre, are one of the joys of life. You can try any extra flavourings you like, try adding subtle spices for an Indian-style croquette or feta cheese and dill for a more Mediterranean flavour.

MAKES **8**
5 MINUTES TO MAKE
10–15 MINUTES TO COOK

200G BABY SPINACH

ABOUT 300G LEFTOVER BEST EVER
MASHED POTATO (PAGE 117)

1 FREE-RANGE EGG YOLK, PLUS 1 FREE-
RANGE EGG, BEATEN, TO COAT

75G BLUE CHEESE, SUCH AS
GORGONZOLA, DOLCELATTE OR
STILTON, CRUMBLED

SEA SALT AND FRESHLY GROUND
BLACK PEPPER

100G BREADCRUMBS

SUNFLOWER OIL, TO FRY

POTATO + BLUE CHEESE CROQUETTES

1. To wilt the spinach, stand a colander in the sink, add the leaves and pour a kettle of boiling water over them. Refresh under cold water then squeeze out as much water as you can with your hands. Chop and put in a bowl.

2. Add the potato, egg yolk and cheese to the bowl, mix well and check the seasoning. Shape into 8 even-sized croquettes, balls or patties. Dip in the beaten egg then coat in breadcrumbs.

3. Heat about 4–5cm of oil in a deep pan and fry the croquettes (in batches if necessary) for 3–4 minutes until golden on all sides. Serve warm.

tip Cook 300g potatoes in boiling salted water and mash well then cool if you don't have any leftover Best Ever Mashed Potato (page 117).

Beetroot with its lovely earth flavour needs very little adornment. It loves an aniseed flavour so dill and tarragon are particular friends of the sweet beet.

BAKED BEETROOT WITH SOURED CREAM + HERBS

SERVES **4**, PLUS LEFTOVERS
10 MINUTES TO MAKE
40 MINUTES TO COOK

1KG SMALL OR MEDIUM BEETROOT, SCRUBBED AND CUT INTO WEDGES

2 TABLESPOONS OLIVE OIL

1 TEASPOON CUMIN SEEDS

SEA SALT AND FRESHLY GROUND BLACK PEPPER

100ML SOURED CREAM

A HANDFUL OF CHOPPED DILL

A HANDFUL OF CHOPPED FLAT-LEAF PARSLEY

50G CHOPPED TOASTED WALNUTS

1. Preheat the oven to 200°C/fan 180°C/gas 6. Tumble the beetroot into a roasting tin and toss with the olive oil and cumin seeds. Season and roast for 40 minutes until tender.

2. Stir through the soured cream with a splash of warm water, add the herbs and spoon into a dish. Sprinkle with the chopped walnuts and serve.

tip Toast the walnuts in a dry frying pan or in the oven for 4 minutes at 160°C/fan 140°C/gas 3 until golden. Watch very carefully as they will burn very quickly.

ENOUGH LEFT OVER FOR:
BEETROOT PILAF (PAGE 122)
BEETROOT + FETA CAKE (PAGE 124) »———→

Ever versatile, a pilaf is the perfect way to breath new life into your leftovers. I would tend to choose rice over pasta as my go-to store cupboard staple, its tender grains feel lighter and more nourishing when you are looking for a quick, simple supper.

SERVES **4**
5 MINUTES TO MAKE
15 MINUTES TO COOK

250G LONG GRAIN RICE

1 TABLESPOON OLIVE OIL

1 LARGE ONION, FINELY CHOPPED

200G GREENS, SLICED (ANY GREEN
 LEAFY VEG WOULD WORK WELL)

300–350G LEFTOVER BAKED BEETROOT
 WITH SOURED CREAM + HERBS
 (PAGE 121), ROUGHLY CHOPPED

100–200G ANY EXTRA BITS YOU HAVE,
 SUCH AS SMOKED FISH, GOAT'S
 CHEESE, LEFTOVER CHICKEN OR
 LAMB (OPTIONAL)

SEA SALT AND FRESHLY GROUND BLACK
 PEPPER

A HANDFUL OF FINELY CHOPPED FLAT-
 LEAF PARSLEY

LEMON JUICE, TO TASTE

BEETROOT PILAF

1. Cook the rice in boiling salted water for 15 minutes until tender.

2. Meanwhile, heat the oil in a pan and fry the onion for 10 minutes until soft and lightly golden. Drain the rice and add to the pan and toss in the fried onion.

3. Blanch the greens briefly in boiling water then drain and add to the rice with the leftover beetroot and any other bits you have. Season and add the parsley and lemon juice to taste and serve.

tip Grate 150g beetroot and gently fry in a little butter and splash of stock or water until tender then add to your pilaf if you don't have any leftover Baked Beetroot (page 121).

The Scandi flavours of the Baked Beetroot with Soured Cream + Herbs (page 121) work strangely well with Greek feta, which is another lover of aniseed – think chilled glasses of ouzo in the warm Aegean sunshine with sharp and tangy feta salads.

SERVES **4**
10 MINUTES TO MAKE
15 MINUTES TO COOK

BEETROOT + FETA CAKE

ABOUT 250G LEFTOVER BAKED
  BEETROOT WITH SOURED CREAM +
  HERBS (PAGE 121)
400G CAN OF CHICKPEAS OR BUTTER
  BEANS, DRAINED AND RINSED
200G FETA, CRUMBLED
2 TABLESPOONS GRAM OR PLAIN
  FLOUR
1 FREE-RANGE EGG
SEA SALT AND FRESHLY GROUND BLACK
  PEPPER
A HANDFUL OF FLAT-LEAF PARSLEY,
  FINELY CHOPPED
SUNFLOWER OIL, FOR FRYING

1. Whizz the beetroot and chickpeas together in a food processor to form a rough paste. Transfer to a bowl and add the feta, flour and egg and mix well. Season and mix in the parsley.

2. Heat a layer of oil in a 20–22cm non-stick frying pan and spoon the mixture into the pan and flatten. Fry for 3–4 minutes until a golden crust has formed. Turn over with a spatula – in quarters if it starts to break up. Fry for a further 3–4 minutes then serve piping hot.

tip If you haven't cooked the Baked Beetroot with Soured Cream + Herbs (page 121) then grate about 200g raw beetroot and mix with a dollop of soured cream and some dill. This would also be wonderful served with a fried or poached egg.

A good potato salad recipe is something that everyone should have in their arsenal. This one is so much more than just a side, full of delicious pickles and onions it's a wonderful meal in itself.

SERVES **4**, PLUS LEFTOVERS
15 MINUTES TO MAKE
15 MINUTES TO COOK

SCANDI POTATO SALAD

1 SMALL RED ONION, FINELY SLICED

1 TABLESPOON RED WINE VINEGAR

1KG NEW POTATOES

SEA SALT AND FRESHLY GROUND BLACK
   PEPPER

½ CUCUMBER, DESEEDED AND FINELY
   DICED

1 BUNCH OF SPRING ONIONS, FINELY
   SLICED

5–6 LARGE DILL PICKLES, FINELY SLICED

2 TEASPOONS DIJON OR ENGLISH
   MUSTARD

4 TABLESPOONS SOURED CREAM

2 TABLESPOONS MAYONNAISE

2 TABLESPOONS GREEK OR NATURAL
   YOGURT

A HANDFUL OF DILL, FINELY CHOPPED

1. Put the onion in a little bowl, pour over the vinegar and set aside.

2. Put the potatoes in a pan of cold, salted water and bring to the boil and simmer for 12–15 minutes until tender. Drain and slice in half or quarter if large.

3. Tip the potatoes into a bowl and add the remaining ingredients. Season well and serve warm or at room temperature scattered with the onions.

ENOUGH LEFT OVER FOR:
POTATO SALAD ROASTIES (PAGE 128)
FRITTATA (PAGE 129) ⟶

When thinking about fun things to do with leftover potato salad, the thought struck me that it could be fun to try roasting it up. It seemed like a bonkers idea but the result was wonderful! Tender and crunchy with a tangy flavour from the rest of the ingredients.

SERVES **4**
5 MINUTES TO MAKE
1 HOUR TO COOK

POTATO SALAD ROASTIES

400G LEFTOVER SCANDI POTATO SALAD
(PAGE 125)
2 TABLESPOONS OLIVE OIL
150G RASHERS OF STREAKY BACON OR
PANCETTA, CHOPPED

1. Preheat the oven to 200°C/fan 180°C/gas 6. Tip the leftover potato salad into a roasting tin, drizzle with the oil and roast for 30 minutes. Turn and scatter with the bacon bits and roast for a further 25–30 minutes until all is crispy.

tip If you haven't made the Scandi Potato Salad (page 125), cook 400g new potatoes and toss with olive oil and a good tablespoon each of mayonnaise and yogurt and a few chopped pickled gherkins or cornichons before roasting.

Eggs make the best quick supper and are a great foil for lots of different flavours so a frittata is one of the most satisfying simple dishes you can cook on a shoestring.

SERVES **4** AS A LUNCH
10 MINUTES TO MAKE
15 MINUTES TO COOK

FRITTATA

6 EGGS
250G LEFTOVER SCANDI POTATO SALAD
   (PAGE 125)
100–150G CHEESE, SUCH AS FETA,
   MOZZARELLA, PARMESAN OR
   RICOTTA, CRUMBLED OR GRATED IF
   NECESSARY
A HANDFUL OF CHOPPED FLAT-LEAF
   PARSLEY
SEA SALT AND FRESHLY GROUND BLACK
   PEPPER
A LITTLE OIL OR BUTTER

1. Whisk the eggs in a bowl. Slice up the leftover Scandi Potato Salad and add to the bowl with the cheese and parsley. Season well.

2. Preheat the grill to medium. Gently heat a smidge of oil or butter in a 20–23cm non-stick frying pan over a low heat and pour in the mixture. Cook for 12–15 minutes until just set then pop the pan under the grill for 30 seconds to golden up the top. Serve warm or at room temperature.

tip Without any leftover Scandi Potato Salad (page 125), cook 250g new potatoes until tender, drain and toss with a dollop of mayonnaise and a dollop of yogurt and some olive oil. Add a few sliced gherkins or cornichons and a little bit of Dijon mustard then leave to cool.

Braised cabbage is not just for Christmas, take comfort in the slow cooking process as crunchy vibrant raw cabbage slowly mellows and sweetens as it becomes tender in the pot.

SERVES 4, PLUS LEFTOVERS
5 MINUTES TO MAKE
1½ HOURS TO COOK

BRAISED RED CABBAGE

1 RED ONION, FINELY SLICED

1 LARGE RED CABBAGE, FINELY SLICED,
   CORE REMOVED

1 DESSERT APPLE, QUARTERED, CORED,
   PEELED AND GRATED

3 TABLESPOONS SOFT LIGHT BROWN
   SUGAR

60ML RED WINE VINEGAR, CIDER
   VINEGAR OR MALT VINEGAR

125ML DRY CIDER OR APPLE JUICE

1 CINNAMON STICK

SEA SALT AND FRESHLY GROUND BLACK
   PEPPER

1. Put all the ingredients into a large, heavy-based pan or flameproof casserole with a lid. Add a splash of water and bring to a simmer. Reduce the heat as low as possible and cook, covered, for 1–1 ½ hours until the cabbage is really tender, stirring occasionally. Season and serve.

ENOUGH LEFT OVER FOR:
RED CABBAGE CHUTNEY (PAGE 132)
MIXED PICKLED BRASSICA SLAW (PAGE 134) »⟶

A good chutney like this is worth its weight in gold for the transformation it makes to a plate of bread and cheese.

MAKES 2 X 400ML JARS
15 MINUTES TO MAKE
45 MINUTES TO COOK

ABOUT 400G LEFTOVER BRAISED RED
    CABBAGE (PAGE 131)
2 APPLES, SUCH AS COX, GRATED
A HANDFUL OF DRIED FRUIT, SUCH
    AS APRICOTS, PRUNES, SULTANAS OR
    RAISINS, CHOPPED IF LARGE
1 TEASPOON EACH YELLOW MUSTARD
    SEEDS, GROUND TURMERIC, CUMIN
    SEEDS AND CHILLI FLAKES
100G PRESERVING SUGAR
175ML RED WINE VINEGAR

RED CABBAGE CHUTNEY

1. Put all the ingredients into a heavy-based pan, bring to a simmer and cook for 30–45 minutes until thickened and fragrant. Spoon into warm, sterilised jars and seal. Mature for a week in a cool, dark place before using. Once opened keep in the fridge.

tips If you don't have the leftover Braised Red Cabbage (page 131), simply start with about 400g raw cabbage instead and cook for an extra 20–30 minutes.

To sterilise your jars, wash well in hot soapy water, rinse, then put in a low oven (110°C/fan 90°C/gas ¼) to completely dry out. Or you could just put them on a hot wash in your dishwasher.

There is something really pleasing about the mix of textures in this slaw, where crunchy gives way to soft and yielding.

SERVES **4**

10 MINUTES TO MAKE.
PLUS MARINATING

200-250G LEFTOVER BRAISED RED
   CABBAGE (PAGE 131)

500G OTHER BRASSICAS, SUCH AS
   WHITE CABBAGE, POINTY CABBAGE,
   SAVOY OR KALE, FINELY SLICED

2 CARROTS, CUT INTO THIN LONG
   MATCHSTICKS

1 APPLE, SUCH AS COX, PEELED AND
   COARSELY GRATED

100ML CIDER VINEGAR

50G CASTER SUGAR

1 TABLESPOONS YELLOW MUSTARD
   SEEDS

2-3 TABLESPOONS SOURED CREAM,
   GREEK OR NATURAL YOGURT

EXTRA VIRGIN OLIVE OIL, TO DRIZZLE

MIXED PICKLED BRASSICA SLAW

1. Mix the leftover red cabbage with the other vegetables and apple in a large bowl and set aside. Heat the vinegar with the sugar and mustard seeds over a low heat until the sugar has melted. Pour the hot vinegar over the vegetables and toss together. Set aside for 20 minutes then add the soured cream or yogurt and some extra virgin olive oil and seasoning and serve.

tip If you don't have any leftover Braised Red Cabbage (page 131), you can either make this recipe with 300g sliced raw red cabbage or fry the cabbage in a little butter with a good splash of cider and a little vinegar for 10-15 minutes until softened slightly.

One of my favourite dishes has to be aubergine parmigiana but I was feeling a bit lazy and the thought of frying up aubergines and making sauce was a bit more than I felt like doing. So here is my quick version, all the flavour and the oven does all the work.

ROAST AUBERGINE + TOMATOES

SERVES **4**, PLUS LEFTOVERS
5 MINUTES TO MAKE
50 MINUTES TO COOK

3 AUBERGINES, CUT INTO CHUNKS

300G VINE TOMATOES, HALVED

1 BULB GARLIC, CLOVES SEPARATED

OLIVE OIL

SEA SALT AND FRESHLY GROUND BLACK
   PEPPER

2 BALLS BUFFALO MOZZARELLA, TORN

BASIL LEAVES, TO SCATTER

CRUSTY BREAD, TO SERVE

1. Preheat the oven to 180°C/fan 160°C/gas 4. Put the aubergines and tomatoes into a roasting tin and scatter in the garlic cloves. Drizzle with lots of olive oil and season well.

2. Roast for 40–45 minutes, turning the aubergine occasionally, until the aubergine is really tender and the tomatoes are soft and golden. Dot the mozzarella all over with and return to the oven for 5–10 minutes. Scatter with basil and serve with crusty bread.

ENOUGH LEFT OVER FOR:
PASTA BAKE WITH AUBERGINE + TOMATOES
   (PAGE 136)
AUBERGINE + TOMATO MINI CALZONE (PAGE 137) ⟶

Sometimes it is the simplest things that are the most satisfying, showing that good food doesn't have to be complicated.

SERVES **4–6**
20 MINUTES TO MAKE
30 MINUTES TO COOK

PASTA BAKE WITH AUBERGINE + TOMATOES

300G SHORT PASTA, SUCH AS FUSILLI, PENNE OR RIGATONI

1 TABLESPOON OLIVE OIL

1 ONION, FINELY SLICED

A GOOD PINCH OF CHILLI FLAKES OR 1 RED OR GREEN CHILLI, FINELY CHOPPED

300G LEFTOVER ROAST AUBERGINE + TOMATOES (PAGE 135)

400G CAN OF CHOPPED TOMATOES

SPLASH OF CREAM, CRÈME FRAÎCHE OR SOURED CREAM

40G PARMESAN CHEESE OR ANY OTHER MELTING CHEESE, SUCH AS COMTE, GRUYÈRE, FONTINA, TALEGGIO OR BRIE

A HANDFUL OF FLAT-LEAF PARSLEY, CHOPPED

1. Preheat the oven to 200°C/fan 180°C/gas 6. Cook the pasta in a pan of boiling salted water according to the packet instructions until almost but not quite cooked.

2. Meanwhile, heat the oil in a pan and gently fry the onion and chilli for 10 minutes until softened. Add the leftover Roast Aubergine + Tomatoes and chopped tomatoes and simmer for 15–20 minutes. Add the cream, crème fraîche or soured cream cheese and parsley then tip the whole lot into an ovenproof dish and bake for 20–25 minutes until the dish is golden.

tip If you haven't made the Roast Aubergine + Tomatoes (page 135), simply fry up an aubergine, sliced or chopped, in olive oil until really soft. Add a squidge of tomato purée to boost the tomato-ey flavour. Tear up a ball of mozzarella and toss through the pasta with the aubergine.

Making your own pizza dough is not only really easy, but great fun and tastes so much better than any pizza you can buy.

MAKES **12** MINI CALZONES
30 MINUTES TO MAKE
15 MINUTES TO COOK

500G STRONG BREAD FLOUR, PLUS
  EXTRA TO DUST
7G SACHET DRIED FAST ACTION YEAST
2 TEASPOONS SALT
2 TABLESPOONS EXTRA VIRGIN OLIVE
  OIL
250G CAN CHOPPED TOMATOES
300G LEFTOVER ROAST AUBERGINE +
  TOMATOES (PAGE 135)
200G CHEESE, SUCH AS PARMESAN,
  MOZZARELLA, BLUE CHEESE OR A MIX
ANY OTHER STORE CUPBOARD
  ADDITIONS, SUCH AS A COUPLE OF
  ANCHOVIES, BLACK OLIVES OR
  ARTICHOKE HEARTS

AUBERGINE + TOMATO MINI CALZONES

1. Mix the flour with the yeast and salt in a bowl. Add the oil and enough lukewarm water to form a soft but not too sticky dough. Knead vigorously for 10 minutes then put the dough in a clean, oiled bowl and cover with clingfilm. Leave to rise in a warm place for an hour or until doubled in size.

2. Meanwhile, heat a pan until really hot, add the canned tomatoes and bubble for 5 minutes to reduce to a thick sauce. Add the leftover aubergine and tomatoes and bubble together for 10 minutes. Remove from the heat and set aside to cool.

3. Remove the dough from the bowl, knead briefly then divide into 12 equal-sized balls. Preheat the oven to its hottest setting.

4. Roll and stretch each ball of dough to a disc about 16–18cm in diameter on a floured surface. Dollop a generous spoon of the aubergine into the middle, scatter with cheese and any other store cupboard additions you want. Brush the edges of the dough with water, fold in half and seal with a little twist, like a Cornish pasty.

5. Slide onto 1–2 baking sheets then bake for 10–12 minutes until golden and crisp on the outside.

tip If you haven't cooked the Roast Aubergine + Tomatoes (page 135), dice an aubergine, drizzle with plenty of oil and roast for 30 minutes until soft. Use this with an extra squidge of tomato purée instead of the leftovers.

There was a bit of debate when photographing this recipe about the difference between a gratin and a dauphinoise. We reached the conclusion that a dauphinoise is a type of gratin and that anything topped with a browned crust is all 'familie gratin'.

ROOT VEGETABLE GRATIN

SERVES **4**, PLUS LEFTOVERS
15 MINUTES TO MAKE
1½ HOURS TO COOK

30G UNSALTED BUTTER

1 ONION

300G FLOURY POTATOES

2 PARSNIPS

1 CELERIAC

A HANDFUL OF THYME SPRIGS, LEAVES
   STRIPPED

2 TABLESPOONS PLAIN FLOUR

SEA SALT AND FRESHLY GROUND BLACK
   PEPPER

300ML CHICKEN (PAGE 19) OR
   VEGETABLE STOCK

400ML DOUBLE CREAM

A HANDFUL OF FRESH OR DRIED
   BREADCRUMBS

50G CHEDDAR CHEESE, GRATED

1. Preheat the oven to 180°C/fan 160°C/gas 4. Rub the butter all over the inside of 1.2-litre ovenproof dish. Peel and finely slice all the vegetables and toss together with the thyme, flour and plenty of seasoning. Tumble into the dish.

2. Mix the stock and cream together and pour over the vegetables then mix the breadcrumbs and cheese together and scatter over the top. Bake for 1½ hours until the vegetables are tender and the top golden and bubbling.

ENOUGH LEFT OVER FOR:
GRATIN HASH WITH POACHED EGGS (PAGE 140)
SAVOURY GRATIN MUFFINS (PAGE 142) »⟶

I don't know what it is about a hash that is so completely satisfying and glorious – I think it is because I love anything that I can eat without a knife! This comforting, creamy hash is a true winter wonder.

GRATIN HASH WITH POACHED EGGS

SERVES **4**
20 MINUTES TO MAKE
25 MINUTES TO COOK

1 TABLESPOON OLIVE OIL

1 ONION, FINELY CHOPPED

100G BACON, CHORIZO OR SALAMI, FINELY CHOPPED

2 GARLIC CLOVES, CRUSHED

400G LEFTOVER ROOT VEGETABLE GRATIN (PAGE 139)

A HANDFUL OF SOFT HERBS, SUCH AS FLAT-LEAF PARSLEY, TARRAGON OR BASIL, CHOPPED

4 FREE-RANGE EGGS

SEA SALT AND FRESHLY GROUND BLACK PEPPER

1. Heat the oil in a frying pan and gently fry the onion for 10 minutes until softened. Add the bacon and fry for 10 minutes until it is starting to crisp. Add the garlic and cook for 30 seconds then add the leftover gratin and herbs, crushing slightly with a fork to flatten the gratin in the base of the pan.

2. Cook over a medium–low heat for 5–6 minutes until golden and brown on the bottom then turn over with a spatula – don't worry if it breaks up a bit, just squash it back down again. Cook for a further 5–6 minutes until the other side is golden.

3. Meanwhile, bring a pan of water to the boil then reduce the heat until the water is just simmering. Poach the eggs gently for 4 minutes.

4. Serve scoops of the hash with the softly poached eggs, plenty of fresh black pepper and a scattering of sea salt.

tips Without the leftover Root Vegetable Gratin (page 139) you can make a slightly different version of this hash. Peel and dice a potato, parsnip and a chunk of celeriac. Simmer in boiling water for a few minutes until tender then drain. Add to the pan and fry up when you would fry the gratin, adding a splash of double cream as you go.

Remember the best poached eggs are made from the freshest ones, so go for one as straight from the hen as you can!

A savoury gratin muffin is so much more versatile than the sweet kind. A fabulous breakfast on the go or a simple lunch warm from the oven with a glass of cold beer or cider.

MAKES **12**
15 MINUTES TO MAKE
18 MINUTES TO COOK

350G LEFTOVER ROOT VEGETABLE
   GRATIN (PAGE 139)
5 MEDIUM FREE-RANGE EGGS,
   SEPARATED
150G SELF-RAISING FLOUR
60ML WHOLE MILK
30G UNSALTED BUTTER, MELTED
100G GRATED CHEESE, SUCH AS
   CHEDDAR, PARMESAN OR GRUYÈRE
1 BUNCH OF CHIVES OR SPRING
   ONIONS, FINELY CHOPPED

SAVOURY GRATIN MUFFINS

1. Preheat the oven to 200°C/fan 180°C/gas 6 and line a 12-hole muffin tin with paper cases.

2. Mash the leftover gratin with a fork. Whisk the egg yolks and flour together then whisk in the milk and add the mashed gratin, melted butter, cheese and chives or spring onions.

3. Whisk the egg whites in a clean bowl until holding stiff peaks and gently fold them into the gratin mixture until just combined. Divide between the muffin cases and bake for 15–18 minutes until risen and golden. Leave to cool in the tin then serve warm.

tip If you don't have any leftover Root Vegetable Gratin (page 139), grate a small potato, a small parsnip and a little bit of celeriac. Blanch briefly in boiling salted water then drain well and pat dry. Mix with a little double cream and plenty of seasoning and use 300g of this mixture instead of the leftover gratin.

So often tomato sauces are thin and watery or too sharp and raw-tasting. The key is in the roasting, the tomatoes slow cook and start to dry out, becoming sweeter and more intense before you turn them into the best tomato sauce you have ever tasted.

SERVES 4, PLUS LEFTOVERS
10 MINUTES TO MAKE
1 HOUR 10 MINUTES TO COOK

BEST EVER TOMATO SAUCE

1.5KG RIPE VINE TOMATOES, HALVED
60ML OLIVE OIL, PLUS EXTRA TO DRIZZLE
SEA SALT AND FRESHLY GROUND BLACK PEPPER
3 GARLIC CLOVES, FINELY SLICED
2 TEASPOONS SHERRY VINEGAR
PINCH OF CASTER SUGAR

1. Preheat the oven to 200°C/fan 180°C/gas 6. Place the tomatoes in a large roasting tin and drizzle with a little olive oil and season with plenty of sea salt and freshly ground black pepper. Roast for 30–40 minutes.

2. Heat the remaining 60ml oil in a saucepan, add the garlic and infuse very gently over a low heat for a minute then set aside.

3. Once the tomatoes are really soft and tender, add them to the infused oil. Heat gently, crushing the tomatoes with a fork. Add the vinegar and sugar and bubble for 20–30 minutes until you have a thick, rich sauce.

4. Serve with freshly cooked pasta and lots of grated Parmesan.

ENOUGH LEFT OVER FOR:
VEGGIE RISSOLES IN TOMATO SAUCE (PAGE 146)
POTATO + HALLOUMI IN SPICED TOMATO SAUCE (PAGE 147) »—→

I love the word rissole, it's so wonderfully old-fashioned, and these are lovely little fried balls of goodness smothered in a deliciously rich tomato sauce.

SERVES 4
5 MINUTES TO MAKE
15 MINUTES TO COOK

VEGGIE RISSOLES IN TOMATO SAUCE

300G GRATED COURGETTES OR A MIX OF COURGETTES, CARROTS, POTATOES OR OTHER VEGETABLES

2 FREE-RANGE EGGS, BEATEN

1 SMALL ONION, RED ONION OR A FEW SPRING ONIONS, FINELY CHOPPED

8 TABLESPOONS PLAIN FLOUR

250G MIXED GRATED CHEESE, SUCH AS PARMESAN, CHEDDAR, FETA, MOZZARELLA OR GRUYÈRE

SEA SALT AND FRESHLY GROUND BLACK PEPPER

SUNFLOWER OIL, TO FRY

200-300ML LEFTOVER BEST EVER TOMATO SAUCE (PAGE 145)

A HANDFUL OF SOFT HERBS, SUCH AS BASIL, PARSLEY OR TARRAGON, CHOPPED

1. Mix the grated vegetables with the eggs, onion, plain flour and cheese and some seasoning. Shape into 10 little balls.

2. Heat a little oil in a non-stick frying pan and fry the rissoles for 5–6 minutes until golden and crisp. Warm the leftover tomato sauce in a saucepan over a medium heat, add the rissoles then bubble for a minute, scatter with the herbs and serve.

tip Without the leftover Best Ever Tomato Sauce (page 146) you can make a quick version. Heat a pan over a high heat and add a tin of cherry tomatoes so that they splutter and fizz. Mash up and add a little splash of water and plenty of seasoning and cook for 10-15 minutes until thickend and reduced. Add a good glug of extra virgin olive oil, 1–2 teaspoons of red wine vinegar and a finely sliced garlic clove and simmer for a further minute or two.

Squeaky cheese is an apt name for this semi-soft Cypriot cheese, which bounces and squeaks delightfully between the teeth as it starts to cool. It has a wonderful sharp flavour but goes perfectly with the leftover Best Ever Tomato Sauce.

SERVES **4**
15 MINUTES TO MAKE
20 MINUTES TO COOK

POTATO + HALLOUMI IN SPICED TOMATO SAUCE

TABLESPOON SUNFLOWER OIL
1 RED ONION, FINELY CHOPPED
1 CHILLI, FINELY CHOPPED OR
   1 TEASPOON CHILLI FLAKES
300–400ML LEFTOVER BEST EVER
   TOMATO SAUCE (PAGE 145)
500G NEW POTATOES, SWEET
   POTATOES OR SQUASH, SLICED OR
   CUT INTO CHUNKS
200G FROZEN PEAS, BROAD BEANS OR
   EDAMAME
225G HALLOUMI, PANEER,
   KEFALOTYRI OR KASSERI, THICKLY
   SLICED INTO 8 PIECES
A HANDFUL OF SOFT HERBS, BASIL,
   FLAT-LEAF PARSLEY OR TARRAGON
   CHOPPED

1. Heat the sunflower oil in a non-stick pan and gently fry the onion and chilli for 10 minutes until lovely and soft. Add the tomato sauce, a splash of water and the sliced potatoes or squash and simmer gently, covered, for 15–20 minutes until the potatoes are completely tender. Add the peas and simmer for a further minute or two.

2. Heat a pan over a high heat and fry the slices of cheese for 1–2 minutes, turning once, until golden on both sides.

3. Stir the herbs through the potatoes. Serve the fried cheese with the potatoes and sauce.

tip Without the leftover Best Ever Tomato Sauce (page 145) you can make a quick version of this dish. Heat a pan over a high heat and add a tin of cherry tomatoes so that they splutter and fizz. Mash up and add a little splash of water and plenty of seasoning and cook for 10–15 minutes until thickend and reduced. Add a good glug of extra virgin olive oil, 1–2 teaspoons of red wine vinegar and a finely sliced garlic clove and simmer for a further minute or two.

I don't hold truck with anyone who tries to say that a salad is not filling or a meal in itself, after all, a salad is simply a collection of ingredients tossed together with a dressing so anything goes and this one is packed full of all the wonderful flavours of spring.

SPRING VEGETABLE +RICOTTA SALAD

SERVES 4, PLUS LEFTOVERS
15 MINUTES TO MAKE
15 MINUTES TO COOK

300G JERSEY ROYALS OR OTHER NEW
   POTATOES
12 SPEARS ASPARAGUS
150G FRESH PEAS
150G PODDED BABY BROAD BEANS
150G RADISHES, HALVED
400G MIXED LETTUCES AND
   LEAVES, SUCH AS COS, BUTTER,
   RADICCHIO, ROCKET AND
   WATERCRESS, TORN
150G FIRM RICOTTA, CRUMBLED

FOR THE DRESSING
JUICE OF 1 LEMON
2 TEASPOONS DIJON MUSTARD
½ TEASPOONS HONEY
SEA SALT AND FRESHLY GROUND BLACK
   PEPPER
5 TABLESPOONS EXTRA VIRGIN
   OLIVE OIL

1. Put the potatoes in a pan of cold, salted water, bring to the boil and simmer for 15 minutes or until tender. Drain, thickly slice and tip into a bowl.

2. For the dressing, whisk the lemon juice with the mustard and honey and plenty of seasoning then whisk in the olive oil. Pour half the dressing over the warm potatoes.

3. Blanch the asparagus, peas and broad beans in boiling water for a couple of minutes then drain and cool under cold running water. Slice the asparagus and double pod the broad beans and add to the potatoes.

4. Finely slice the radishes and add to the bowl with the remaining ingredients. Pour over the other half of the dressing, toss together and serve.

tip Use any of your favourite lettuce and salad leaves in this recipe, bright, fresh green spring flavours are all beautiful together so mix and match.

ENOUGH LEFT OVER FOR:
SALAD FRY-UP (PAGE 150)
GREEN DIP (PAGE 152) »⟶

Another slightly bizarre idea came about when trying to think what on earth one can do with leftover salad apart from feed it to the chickens or add it to your compost. I started to think about what would happen if you add heat – a bit like braised lettuce and peas – and it turns out it's something wonderful.

SERVES **4**

5 MINUTES TO MAKE

10 MINUTES TO COOK

SALAD FRY-UP

1 TABLESPOON OLIVE OIL

100G BACON, CHORIZO, SALAMI, PARMA HAM, LEFTOVER ROAST MEAT OR SAUSAGES, CHOPPED

2 SLICES OF BREAD, CUT INTO LITTLE CUBES (STALE IS BEST)

300G LEFTOVER SPRING VEGETABLE + RICOTTA SALAD (PAGE 149)

PARMESAN SHAVINGS, TO SERVE

1. Heat the oil in a frying pan or wok and fry the bacon or other meaty bits for 5–6 minutes until crispy. Add the bread cubes and gently fry for 6–8 minutes until golden and crispy then add the salad and toss together until the leaves wilt and everything is warm. Serve with Parmesan shavings.

tip If you haven't made the Spring Vegetable + Ricotta Salad (page 149), you can just add a mixture of different leaves, peas and beans to your pan when you are frying up. Add a little drizzle of vinegar for a nice tang.

I'm a complete sucker for crisps, breadsticks, fingers of toast, anything that you can dunk into a rich, flavourful bowl of homemade dip. I always find that when you open the fridge, you can pretty much always rustle up a dip. This one uses up the bits and pieces that would ordinarily be thrown away.

SERVES **4**

15 MINUTES TO MAKE

GREEN DIP

200G LEFTOVER SPRING VEGETABLE +
 RICOTTA SALAD (PAGE 149),
 ESPECIALLY PEAS, BEANS, ASPARAGUS
1 GARLIC CLOVE, CRUSHED
A COUPLE OF DOLLOPS OF GREEK
 YOGURT, CRÈME FRAÎCHE, SOURED
 CREAM OR CREAM CHEESE OR A MIX
 OF ANY
PARMESAN, GRATED
EXTRA VIRGIN OLIVE OIL, TO DRIZZLE
SEA SALT AND FRESHLY GROUND BLACK
 PEPPER
BREADSTICKS OR TORTILLA CHIPS,
 TO SERVE

1. Whizz the leftover salad in a small food processor, add enough yogurt to loosen and form a thick paste. Add the Parmesan and a good drizzle of olive oil. If it is too thick, loosen with a little cold water. Check the seasoning and serve with breadsticks or tortilla chips.

tip If you don't have any leftover Spring Vegetable + Ricotta Salad (page 149), cook 150g peas, beans, asparagus or other spring veg, cool under cold running water. Toss with a few leaves with a little lemon and Dijon mustard and whizz with the remaining ingredients.

The autumn brings wonderful displays of beautiful pumpkins and squash with their firm flesh and edible skins. This is a vibrant and delicious dish either as a side or a main meal.

BAKED SQUASH WITH CHILLI + ROSEMARY

SERVES **4**, PLUS LEFTOVERS
10 MINUTES TO MAKE
45 MINUTES TO COOK

2KG SQUASH OR PUMPKIN, DESEEDED
   AND CUT INTO WEDGES
1 BULB GARLIC, CLOVES SEPARATED
2 RED CHILLIES, FINELY SLICED
4 SPRIGS OF ROSEMARY
OLIVE OIL, TO DRIZZLE
1 TABLESPOON CIDER VINEGAR
SEA SALT AND FRESHLY GROUND BLACK
   PEPPER
SEVERAL HANDFULS OF BABY LEAVES,
   TO SERVE

1. Preheat the oven to 200°C/fan 180°C/gas 6. Tumble the squash, garlic, chillies and rosemary into a roasting tin. Drizzle with plenty of olive oil and add the vinegar. Season with lots of sea salt and black pepper and roast for 40–45 minutes until tender. Toss with the baby leaves and serve.

ENOUGH LEFT OVER FOR:
SQUASH + PARMESAN SOUFFLÉ (PAGE 156)
SQUASH LASAGNE (PAGE 157) »⟶

Soufflés, they cast fear into the heart of many cooks, but in reality they are much more robust and simple to make than you would imagine. In the past I have even removed a soufflé from the oven, dug into the centre, realised it is not quite cooked and stuck it back in to finish.

SQUASH + PARMESAN SOUFFLÉ

SERVES **4**
20 MINUTES TO MAKE
25–30 MINUTES TO COOK

50G UNSALTED BUTTER, PLUS EXTRA
   FOR GREASING
A HANDFUL OF FRESH OR DRIED
   BREADCRUMBS, POLENTA OR
   SEMOLINA
40G PLAIN FLOUR
300ML WHOLE MILK
SEA SALT AND FRESHLY GROUND BLACK
   PEPPER
4 FREE-RANGE EGGS, SEPARATED
200–250G LEFTOVER BAKED SQUASH
   WITH CHILLI + ROSEMARY (PAGE 153),
   MASHED WITH A FORK
100G PARMESAN CHEESE OR ANY
   OTHER CHEESE, GRATED

1. Preheat the oven to 200°C/fan 180°C/gas 6 and grease a deep 20cm soufflé dish with butter and then coat with a thin layer of breadcrumbs, polenta or semolina to help the mixture climb up the sides of the dish.

2. Melt the butter in a saucepan then add the flour and cook for a couple of minutes. Add the milk a little at a time, stirring to create a smooth sauce. Season and bubble for a minute or two.

3. Remove from the heat and stir in the egg yolks, mashed squash and Parmesan. Whisk the egg whites in a clean bowl until holding stiff peaks. Mix a dollop into the béchamel sauce then gently fold in the remaining egg whites. Fill the soufflé dish to just below the top.

4. Place on a baking sheet and bake for 25–30 minutes until well risen and golden.

tip Without leftover Baked Squash with Chilli + Rosemary (page 153), quickly peel 250g squash or pumpkin and steam for 10-15 minutes until softened. Mash. Heat a pan with a little oil and fry ½ finely chopped red chilli and 1 finely sliced garlic clove then mix through the mashed squash. Cool and use in the soufflé.

The rich tang of goat's cheese is completely delicious with squash, you won't miss the ragù in this gorgeous quick veggie lasagne.

SERVES **4**

20 MINUTES TO MAKE

35 MINUTES TO COOK

SQUASH LASAGNE

30G UNSALTED BUTTER

30G PLAIN FLOUR

350ML WHOLE MILK

SEA SALT AND FRESHLY GROUND BLACK
  PEPPER

6 FRESH LASAGNE SHEETS OR ANY
  PASTA, BLANCHED

300-400G LEFTOVER BAKED SQUASH
  WITH CHILLI + ROSEMARY (PAGE 153),
  ROUGHLY CHOPPED

150G GREENS OR SPINACH, SHREDDED
  AND WILTED

60G HARD GOAT'S CHEESE, CHEDDAR
  OR BLUE CHEESE, PARMESAN OR A
  MIX, GRATED

1. Preheat the oven to 200°C/fan 180°C/gas 6. Melt the butter in a pan then add the flour and cook over a medium heat for a minute or two. Add the milk gradually, stirring constantly, until you have a thick glossy sauce. Season well.

2. Put a little of the béchamel into the bottom of a 1.2–1.5-litre ovenproof dish, top with a 2 lasagne sheets then half the squash and blanched greens then repeat, ending with the remaining lasagne sheets and a layer of the béchamel. Scatter over the cheese and bake for 25–30 minutes until golden.

tip If you have no leftover Baked Squash with Chilli + Rosemary (page 153), while you make the sauce roast 400g diced squash tossed in oil with a little chilli and garlic until softened and then use this in the recipe.

VANILLA CRÈME ANGLAISE
MOUSSELINE ICING
PORTUGUESE CUSTARD TARTS

HOT LEMON SPONGE PUDDING
LEMON FANCIES
LEMON + RASPBERRY LAYERS

MARMALADE
OATY MARMALADE BITES
STICKY MARMALADE CAKE

BERRY COMPOTE
BERRY + LIME POTS
BERRY RIPPLE ICE CREAM

APPLE + PECAN CRUMBLE
CRUMBLE CUPCAKES
APPLE + PECAN CRUMBLE TART

STAR ANISE + HONEY POACHED PEARS
PEAR TARTE FINE
UPSIDE DOWN PEAR + ALMOND CAKES

STICKY ALMOND + HONEY TART
SEMIFREDDO SLICE
STUFFED BAKED APPLES

CARDAMOM + CINNAMON BUNS
CARDAMOM BUN + CREAM PUDDING
PAIN PERDU

RICH CHOCOLATE MOUSSE
MINI CHOC 'N' NUT ICE CREAMS
CHOCOLATE FRIDGE CAKE

SWEET

My favourite pudding when I was younger was cold banana custard – and my love of custard has never dimmed. If I am honest I like my custard on its own with a spoon but I realise most other people prefer it with pudding!

SERVES **4**, PLUS LEFTOVERS
5 MINUTES TO MAKE
20 MINUTES TO COOK

VANILLA CRÈME ANGLAISE

300ML WHOLE MILK
300ML DOUBLE CREAM
1 VANILLA POD, SPLIT
4 FREE-RANGE EGG YOLKS
50G CASTER SUGAR
1 TEASPOON CORNFLOUR

1. Pour the milk and cream into a saucepan, scrape the seeds from the vanilla pod and add to the pan with the pod itself. Heat until almost boiling.

2. Meanwhile, beat the egg yolks, sugar and cornflour together in a heatproof bowl until smooth, pour the hot milk over and stir well. Clean the pan and return the mixture to it.

3. Cook over a low heat, stirring constantly with a wooden spoon, until the mixture thickens and coats the back of the spoon.

tip Serve with tarts, such as the Sticky Almond + Honey Tart (page 191), pies, crumbles and steamed puddings like the Hot Lemon Sponge Pudding on page 167.

ENOUGH LEFT OVER FOR:
MOUSSELINE ICING (PAGE 162)
PORTUGUESE CUSTARD TARTS (PAGE 164) ⇥⟶

Having made many wedding cakes in my time I am always searching for the ultimate icing – rich and sweet but stable and not cloying. I think this is it.

MOUSSELINE ICING

MAKES ENOUGH TO ICE 20CM
CAKE (INSIDE AND OUT)
25 MINUTES TO MAKE

2 EGG WHITES
100G ICING SUGAR
125G UNSALTED BUTTER, SOFTENED
100ML LEFTOVER VANILLA CRÈME
ANGLAISE (PAGE 161)

1. Put the egg whites and icing sugar in a heatproof bowl and place over a pan of simmering water. Whisk with a hand whisk until you have a thick meringue mixture that holds its shape. Remove from the heat and beat off the heat until cool.

2. In a separate bowl, beat the butter and leftover crème anglaise together until really light and fluffy. Gradually add the meringue, a little at a time, beating in until you have a thick, smooth icing. Use to decorate one 20cm cake or cupcakes.

tip If you didn't make the Vanilla Crème Anglaise (page 161), you can also make a classic mousseline icing using 175g butter and a little vanilla extract.

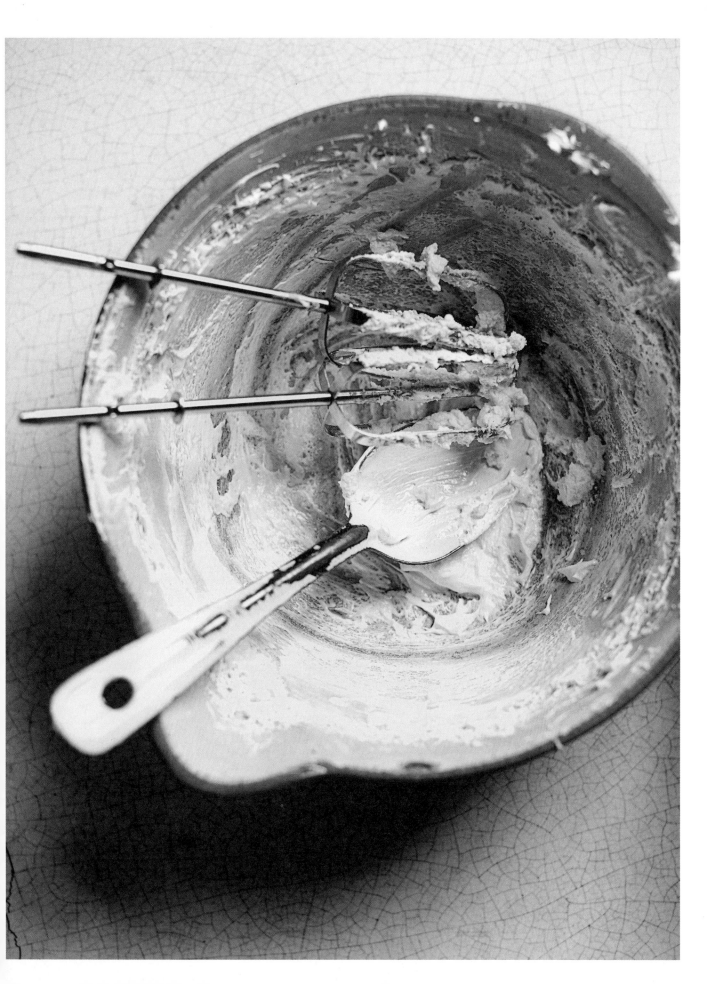

Pastéis de nata are a heavenly mouthful of light, flaky pastry with rich, caramelised custard. This is a cheat's version but just as delicious as the real deal.

250ML LEFTOVER VANILLA CRÈME
   ANGLAISE (PAGE 161)
50ML DOUBLE CREAM
1 TEASPOON CORNFLOUR, PLUS
   EXTRA TO DUST
25G CASTER SUGAR
1 FREE-RANGE EGG
GOOD GRATING OF NUTMEG
320G PACK READY-ROLLED ALL-BUTTER
   PUFF PASTRY

PORTUGUESE CUSTARD TARTS

1. Put the crème anglaise in a bowl and whisk the cream and cornflour together then add to the bowl with the caster sugar, egg and nutmeg.

2. Unroll the puff pastry onto a lightly floured surface and roll out until 2mm thick. Roll the pastry up like a Swiss roll and slice into 12 even pieces.

3. Place each piece on its end (so you can see the rolls) and squash flat. Then put each piece into the hole of a 12-hole muffin tin and push up the sides with your fingers.

4. Preheat the oven to 240°C/fan 220°C/gas 9 or as hot as your oven will go. Pour the custard into the pastry cases then bake for 15–20 minutes until the pastry is cooked and the top starting to scorch. Leave to cool in the tin for a few minutes before removing.

tip If you don't have any leftover Vanilla Crème Anglaise (page 161), you can mix 3 free-range egg yolks with 250g crème fraîche and some vanilla and nutmeg.

I'm not quite sure why steamed puddings have such a dowdy reputation, or why people think they will be leaden and dense. It is true that steaming a cake mixture gives a completely different texture to a traditional baked cake, but it is light, tender and wonderful warm.

HOT LEMON SPONGE PUDDING

SERVES **4**, PLUS LEFTOVERS
15 MINUTES TO MAKE
2 HOURS TO COOK

200G UNSALTED BUTTER, SOFTENED, PLUS EXTRA TO GREASE
FINELY GRATED ZEST AND JUICE OF 3 LEMONS
40G SOFT LIGHT BROWN SUGAR
200G CASTER SUGAR
4 FREE-RANGE EGGS
135G SELF-RAISING FLOUR
65G GROUND ALMONDS
DOUBLE CREAM, TO SERVE

1. Grease a 1.2-litre pudding basin with butter and mix the juice of 2 lemons with the brown sugar in the bottom of the basin.

2. Beat the butter and caster sugar together until really light and fluffy, add the eggs one at a time, beating well between each addition. Fold in the flour, almonds and lemon zest. Finally add the remaining lemon juice.

3. Spoon the sponge mixture into the pudding basin on top of the lemon and sugar mixture. Cover the top of the bowl with a double layer, one of baking parchment and one of foil, with the foil uppermost, and tie with string around the bowl to secure.

4. Put into a deep saucepan and pour boiling water around the outside so it comes halfway up the bowl. Cover and bring to the boil then reduce to a simmer and steam for 2 hours, topping up the boiling water every so often, if necessary.

5. Remove the basin from the pan and take off the foil and paper. Run a knife around the edge of the pudding then turn it out onto a serving plate. Serve scoops of the hot sponge with double cream.

ENOUGH LEFT OVER FOR:
LEMON FANCIES (PAGE 168)
LEMON + RASPBERRY LAYERS (PAGE 170) »⟶

I was nervous about trying to make little fancies out of a steamed sponge, fearing they would fall to pieces, but it turns out the wonderful thing about a steamed sponge is that when it is cold it is compact and not at all crumbly, making it perfect for dipping in prettily coloured fondant icing.

MAKES **6–8**
45 MINUTES TO MAKE

250G LEFTOVER HOT LEMON SPONGE
   PUDDING (PAGE 167)
2–3 TABLESPOONS APRICOT JAM
30G UNSALTED BUTTER, SOFTENED
30G ICING SUGAR
250G FONDANT ICING SUGAR
FOOD COLOURING OF YOUR CHOICE

LEMON FANCIES

1. Cut the sponge into even 2cm squares and brush all over with apricot jam (you may want to warm the jam first).

2. Beat the softened butter with the icing sugar then put into a small piping bag (a disposable one or one with a small plain nozzle) and pipe a small bobble on top of each sponge square. Chill for 30 minutes.

3. Mix the fondant icing sugar with the food colouring and enough water to turn it into a thick, pourable mixture. Take each cake and stand on a wire rack and pour over the fondant icing so it cascades down over each one. Leave to set then serve with a cup of tea.

tip Without the leftover Hot Lemon Sponge Pudding (page 167), you can use a firm madeira cake instead and add some finely grated lemon zest to the butter icing and a squeeze of lemon juice to the fondant instead of water.

I love the way that the leftover sponge pudding soaks up the limoncello, well, like a sponge! Served with generous dollops of cream and the tang of raspberries this is a fabulous twist on a classic trifle.

LEMON + RASPBERRY LAYERS

SERVES **4**

10 MINUTES TO MAKE

250G LEFTOVER HOT LEMON SPONGE PUDDING (PAGE 167), BROKEN OR SLICED

100ML LIMONCELLO, RUM, BRANDY OR SHERRY

4 TABLESPOONS RASPBERRY JAM

300ML DOUBLE CREAM, WHIPPING CREAM OR MASCARPONE

200G FRESH OR FROZEN RASPBERRIES

1. Put the sponge into 4 glasses and drizzle with the booze. Dollop over a little raspberry jam. Whip the cream (or beat the mascarpone) and dollop over the top then scatter with the raspberries and serve.

tip You can make or buy a lemon drizzle cake to make this recipe if you haven't got any leftover Hot Lemon Sponge Pudding (page 167).

Cold, wet January days are designed for the slow cooking of Seville oranges into the wonder that is marmalade. I love my shreds thin, but don't let me tell you how you should enjoy your marmalade! Cut them to however you would like, or even blitz them in a food processor.

MAKES **6** x **350**ML JARS
1 HOUR TO MAKE
2½ HOURS TO COOK

MARMALADE

1KG SEVILLE ORANGES, SCRUBBED
2 LEMONS
1.75KG PRESERVING OR GRANULATED
   SUGAR

1. Halve the fruit and squeeze out all the juice into a large preserving pan. Throw away the lemon skins. Scoop the pulp, pips and pith of the oranges into a muslin square, tie up and add to the pan. Slice the peel into strips, as chunky or as thin as you like and add to the pan.

2. Pour in 2 litres of water and bring to a simmer. Simmer gently for 2 hours, uncovered, until the peel is tender. Put a plate or two in the freezer, to chill for testing.

3. Remove the muslin bag of pips and pith from the pot and set aside to cool. Pour the sugar into the pan and very gently allow the sugar to melt. When the muslin is cool enough, squeeze it out very hard over the pan.

4. Once the sugar has dissolved, increase the heat to a rolling boil and cook ferociously until it reaches setting point. Start testing after about 5 minutes. Remove from the heat, splodge a dollop of marmalade onto a cold plate and return to the freezer for a minute. Then with your finger, push the marmalade. If it wrinkles on the surface then it is ready. If not, return to the heat and boil for a further 5 minutes then test again.

5. Once it has reached setting point, pour into clean sterilised jars (see page 132), seal and leave to cool. Store in a cool, dark place for up to a year. Once opened keep in the fridge for up to a month.

ENOUGH LEFT OVER FOR:
OATY MARMALADE BITES (PAGE 174)
STICKY MARMALADE CAKE (PAGE 175) »——→

I didn't think there was much that could improve a flapjack, that is until I tried adding a generous dollop of homemade marmalade. The bitter tang of the oranges counterbalances the syrupy sweetness of this most classic of teatime treats.

OATY MARMALADE BITES

MAKES **12–16** DEPENDING ON SIZE
10 MINUTES TO MAKE
30 MINUTES TO COOK

150G UNSALTED BUTTER, PLUS EXTRA
    FOR GREASING
125G SOFT LIGHT BROWN SUGAR
4 TABLESPOONS GOLDEN SYRUP
4 TABLESPOONS LEFTOVER
    MARMALADE (PAGE 171)
275G JUMBO PORRIDGE OATS
50G SMALL PORRIDGE OATS

1. Preheat the oven to 180°C/fan 160°C/gas 4. Butter a 21cm cake tin (square or whatever shape you have). Melt the butter with the sugar, syrup and marmalade in a pan over a low heat. Stir in the oats then tip into the tin and press down.

2. Bake for 25–30 minutes until golden and starting to crisp up at the edges. Leave to cool in the tin for 10 minutes then turn out and cut into squares whilst warm.

tip Use shop-bought marmalade if you don't have any homemade (page 171) to hand.

A bright, tangy orange and ginger cake to cheer up any dark day.

SERVES 4
15 MINUTES TO MAKE
25 MINUTES TO COOK

STICKY MARMALADE CAKE

125G UNSALTED BUTTER, SOFTENED,
   PLUS EXTRA TO GREASE
175G LEFTOVER MARMALADE (PAGE 171)
175G SELF-RAISING FLOUR
1 HEAPED TEASPOON GROUND GINGER
130G SOFT LIGHT BROWN SUGAR OR
   CASTER OR DARK BROWN SUGAR
3 FREE-RANGE EGGS
3 PIECES OF STEM GINGER IN SYRUP
   OR CRYSTALLISED GINGER, FINELY
   CHOPPED
A SPLASH OF MILK
CREAM, CUSTARD OR ICE CREAM,
   TO SERVE

1. Preheat the oven to 180°C/fan 160°C/gas 4. Grease a 20cm square cake tin and line with baking parchment. Spread the marmalade over the bottom.

2. Sift the flour and ground ginger into bowl. In a separate bowl, beat the butter and sugar together with an electric hand whisk until really light and fluffy. Add the eggs, one at a time, then add the flour mixture and the stem ginger and any remaining marmalade. Fold together and add a splash of milk to loosen the mixture.

3. Spoon the mixture into the tin and bake for 20–25 minutes until risen and golden. Leave to cool for 5 minutes then turn out, remove the baking parchment and serve with cream, custard or ice cream.

tip If you don't have any homemade marmalade (page 171), use shop-bought instead.

Midsummer brings with it a plethora of wonderful berries, both familiar and unfamiliar. I would say use any berries in this glorious compote, except strawberries – cooked strawberries tend to be mushy and are much better savoured straight from the punnet with cream.

SERVES **4**, PLUS LEFTOVERS
5 MINUTES TO MAKE
10 MINUTES TO COOK

600G MIXED BLACKBERRIES AND
   RASPBERRIES
250G MIXED BLACK, WHITE AND
   REDCURRANTS
60G CASTER SUGAR
1 VANILLA POD, SPLIT IN HALF
   LENGTHWAYS
50ML CRÈME DE CASSIS (OPTIONAL)

BERRY COMPOTE

1. Put all the ingredients into a saucepan and heat gently until the sugar has dissolved then bubble for 10-20 minutes until the fruit has started to break down and release all its juices. Remove from the heat and cool.

2. Serve with yogurt and granola or on top of creamy porridge.

ENOUGH LEFT OVER FOR:
BERRY + LIME POTS (PAGE 178)
BERRY RIPPLE ICE CREAM (PAGE 179) »——→

I love the texture of these little set creams, or possets.
Such a simple dessert but very elegant.

SERVES 4
5 MINUTES TO MAKE
5 MINUTES TO COOK

400ML DOUBLE CREAM
120G CASTER SUGAR
JUICE OF 6 LIMES, PLUS THE ZEST OF 2
150G LEFTOVER BERRY COMPOTE
  (PAGE 177)

BERRY + LIME POTS

1. Put the cream and sugar in a saucepan over a low heat and cook until the sugar has dissolved. Increase the heat and boil for 2-3 minutes then remove from the heat and add the lime juice and zest.

2. Spoon half the mixture into 4 glasses, top with a spoonful of the compote then top with the remaining cream and chill for an hour before serving.

tip Without any leftover Berry Compote, you can simmer 150g mixed berries with 2 tablespoons of caster sugar (or to taste) until softened then cool completely.

On a hot day nothing is nicer than a wafer cone piled high with ice cream. Berry ripple is a particular favourite of mine, although I don't think anything can quite pip mint choc chip to the top spot!

SERVES **4**

30 MINUTES TO MAKE, PLUS
CHILLING AND FREEZING

20 MINUTES TO COOK

400ML WHOLE MILK

6 FREE-RANGE EGG YOLKS

350G CASTER SUGAR

400G LEFTOVER BERRY COMPOTE
(PAGE 177)

600ML DOUBLE CREAM

BERRY RIPPLE ICE CREAM

1. Bring the milk to the boil in a saucepan. In a bowl, whisk the egg yolks and sugar until really pale, fluffy and thick and holding a ribbon when you lift the beaters out.

2. Pour the hot milk over the egg mixture and stir well. Clean the pan and pour the custard mixture back into it. Put over a medium–low heat and cook, stirring, until you have a thick custard that coats the back of a spoon. Leave to cool, cover with clingfilm then chill overnight.

3. Put the leftover compote into a pan and bubble to reduce to a thick, jammy consistency. Set aside to cool.

4. Add the cream to the custard and pour into an ice-cream maker. Churn until frozen. If you don't have an ice-cream maker, pour the mixture into a shallow, freezerproof, lidded container and freeze for 1–2 hours until almost solid, then scrape into a food processor and blend briefly until smooth. Return to the container and freeze once more. Repeat this procedure once or twice until the mixture is very smooth.

5. Scoop the frozen ice cream into a shallow, freezerproof, lidded container, drizzle the compote all over and ripple with a fork. Freeze for at least 6 hours or overnight if possible.

tip Without any leftover Berry Compote, you can simmer 400g mixed berries with 2 tablespoons of caster sugar (or to taste) until softened then increase the heat and bubble until thickened and jammy. Cool completely.

Crumbles are the king of winter comfort puddings, and for good reason. Nestled underneath a golden, nutty crumb is soft and sharp apple, steaming and begging to be smothered with sweet custard.

SERVES **4**, PLUS LEFTOVERS
20 MINUTES TO MAKE
50 MINUTES TO COOK

APPLE + PECAN CRUMBLE

2 BRAMLEY APPLES

5–6 COX APPLES

JUICE OF 1 LEMON

100G CASTER SUGAR

GOOD PINCH OF GROUND CINNAMON

GRATING FRESH NUTMEG

200G UNSALTED BUTTER, CUBED

175G PLAIN FLOUR

150G PECANS, FINELY CHOPPED

75G DEMERARA SUGAR

40G SOFT BROWN SUGAR
   (LIGHT OR DARK)

1 TEASPOON FLAKY SEA SALT

CREAM OR VANILLA ICE CREAM,
   TO SERVE

1. Peel and core the apples, cut into chunks and put in a pie or ovenproof dish. Add the lemon juice, caster sugar, spices and 50g of the butter and mix together.

2. Preheat the oven to 160°C/fan 140°C/gas 3. Toss the remaining butter with the flour and rub together with your fingertips until the mixture resembles breadcrumbs. Add the pecans, demerara and soft brown sugar and salt and mix well then scatter over the top of the apples. Bake for 40–50 minutes until golden and bubbling. Serve with cream or vanilla ice cream.

ENOUGH LEFT OVER FOR:
CRUMBLE CUPCAKES (PAGE 182)
APPLE + PECAN CRUMBLE TART (PAGE 184) »——→

With just a big spoonful of leftover crumble you can make these wonderful teatime cupcakes.

MAKES **9**
30 MINUTES TO MAKE
25 MINUTES TO COOK

150G UNSALTED BUTTER, SOFTENED
150G CASTER SUGAR
3 FREE-RANGE EGGS
125G SELF-RAISING FLOUR
200G LEFTOVER APPLE + PECAN
  CRUMBLE (PAGE 181)
SPLASH OF MILK (OPTIONAL)

FOR THE ICING
3 TABLESPOONS CUSTARD POWDER
100ML DOUBLE CREAM
200G UNSALTED BUTTER OR A MIX
  OF BUTTER, MASCARPONE, CREAM
  CHEESE (ANYTHING FIRM AND
  SPREADABLE)
125G ICING SUGAR

CRUMBLE CUPCAKES

1. Preheat the oven to 180°C/fan 160°C/gas 4 and line 9 holes of a 12-hole muffin tin with paper cases.

2. In a bowl, beat the butter and sugar together until light and fluffy. Add the eggs, one at a time, beating before adding the next one then add the flour and leftover crumble, reserving some to decorate. Fold together, adding a splash of milk if the mixture is too thick.

3. Dollop into the paper cases and bake for 20–25 minutes until golden and risen.

4. Meanwhile, blend the custard powder and cream together in a small pan over a medium–low heat and cook for 2–3 minutes until you have a lovely thick paste. Set aside to cool.

5. Beat the butter (or butter, mascarpone or cream cheese) together with the icing sugar until fluffy. Add the cooled custard mixture and fold in. Chill for at least 30 minutes.

6. When ready to ice, spread the top of each cupcake with some of the icing. Scatter with the reserved crumble and serve.

tip To make these cupcakes from scratch, peel and core 250g Cox apples and cook with a knob of butter, a splash of water and 1 tablespoon of caster sugar for 10 minutes. Use 50g ground almonds instead of the crumble topping in the mix.

Breathe life into yesterday's crumble by transforming it into this showstopping tart.

APPLE + PECAN CRUMBLE TART

SERVES **4**
30 MINUTES TO MAKE
50 MINUTES TO COOK

300ML DOUBLE CREAM

1 TEASPOON VANILLA EXTRACT

3 FREE-RANGE EGG YOLKS

125G CASTER SUGAR

1 TABLESPOON CORNFLOUR

ABOUT 350G LEFTOVER APPLE + PECAN
    CRUMBLE (PAGE 181)

FOR THE PASTRY

275G PLAIN FLOUR, PLUS EXTRA
    TO DUST

180G UNSALTED BUTTER, CHILLED AND
    CUT INTO CUBES

2 TABLESPOONS CASTER SUGAR

1 FREE-RANGE EGG YOLK

1. Heat the cream with the vanilla in a saucepan until almost boiling. Whisk the egg yolks with the sugar and cornflour until smooth. Pour over the hot cream and mix well then return to the pan over a low heat and cook gently for 10–15 minutes until it thickens and coats the back of a spoon. Set aside to cool.

2. To make the tart case, put the flour and butter in a bowl and rub together with your fingertips until the mixture resembles breadcrumbs. Add the sugar followed by the egg yolk and 1–2 tablespoons of cold water and mix with a knife. Bring together with your hands and knead briefly until smooth. Shape into a disc and chill for 10–15 minutes.

3. Preheat the oven to 200°C/fan 180°C/gas 6. Roll the pastry out on a floured surface to 20mm thickness and use to line a 21cm loose-bottomed, fluted tart tin. Line the tin with baking paper and baking beans or rice and blind bake for 15 minutes then remove the paper and beans and bake for a further 4–5 minutes until lightly golden and dry to the touch. Reduce the temperature to 160°C/fan 140°C/gas 3.

4. Carefully remove the crumble from the top of your leftovers. Mix the fruit into the custard and pour into the prepared tart case. Break up the crumble and scatter over the top. Bake for 30 minutes until the custard is set and the top is golden and crunchy.

tip If you don't have any leftover Apple + Pecan Crumble (page 181), peel, core and roughly chop 2 small Cox apples (about 300g) and put in a pan with a knob of butter, 20g caster sugar and a little splash of water. Cook for 10–15 mintues to soften slightly. Rub together 50g butter with 80g plain flour and 1 tablespoon of caster sugar or soft brown sugar and scatter this over the top of your tart.

Poached pears remind me of growing up as my mother would always poach pears for her dinner parties. We were never allowed to eat them until the next day, so to me they are an exotic treat and a leftover rolled into one.

SERVES 4, PLUS LEFTOVERS
10 MINUTES TO MAKE
25 MINUTES TO COOK

ZEST OF 1 ORANGE

ZEST OF 1 LEMON

2 STAR ANISE

2 TABLESPOONS HONEY

1 VANILLA POD, SPLIT

2 X 375ML BOTTLES SWEET DESSERT
   WINE, SUCH AS SAUTERNES

6 RIPE BUT FIRM PEARS, PEELED

STAR ANISE + HONEY POACHED PEARS

1. Put the the fruit zest, star anise, honey and vanilla pod into a large saucepan then pour over the wine and enough water to cover. Bring to the boil and simmer for 5 minutes then add the pears and gently cook for 20-25 minutes until the pears are golden and just tender when prodded with the tip of a sharp knife.

2. Remove the pears with a slotted spoon and transfer to a bowl. Bring the syrup back to the boil then bubble to reduce until about 500ml and slightly syrupy. Cool for 10-15 minutes then pour over the pears and leave to cool completely before serving.

ENOUGH LEFT OVER FOR:
PEAR TARTE FINE (PAGE 188)
UPSIDE DOWN PEAR + ALMOND CAKES
   (PAGE 189) ⇒⟶

A simple and elegant dessert with crisp golden pastry,
soft pears and rich almonds.

SERVES **4**
20 MINUTES TO MAKE
30 MINUTES TO COOK

30G UNSALTED BUTTER, SOFTENED

40G ICING SUGAR

½ TEASPOON VANILLA EXTRACT

1 FREE-RANGE EGG, BEATEN

50G GROUND ALMONDS

½ TEASPOON CORNFLOUR

1 TABLESPOON RUM OR BRANDY

PLAIN FLOUR, TO DUST

375G BLOCK ALL-BUTTER PUFF PASTRY

1–2 LEFTOVER STAR ANISE + HONEY
    POACHED PEARS (PAGE 185)

3 TABLESPOONS APRICOT JAM

PEAR TARTE FINE

1. Preheat the oven to 200°C/fan 180°C/gas 6. Line a baking sheet with baking parchment.

2. Beat the butter, icing sugar and vanilla together until light and fluffy. Add half the egg (reserving the other half to glaze) and beat in then add the almonds, cornflour and rum or brandy.

3. Roll out the pastry on a lightly floured surface until 20mm thick. Cut out a circle about 22cm in diameter. Slide onto the lined baking sheet.

4. Use a knife to score around the edge of your pastry, about 1cm in from the edge to create a border.

5. Spread the almond cream inside the border. Slice and core the pears then slice into thin wedges and place on top of the almond cream. Brush the pastry edge with the reserved beaten egg and bake for 25–30 minutes until golden and puffed.

6. Melt the apricot jam in a pan with 2 teaspoons of water, sieve and return to the pan and bubble for 1–2 minutes until you have a thick glaze. Brush all over the tart and serve.

tip If you haven't cooked the Star Anise + Honey Poached Pears (page 185), slice 2 pears into wedges and use raw.

As a teatime treat or with a good dollop of crème fraiche or cream as a dessert, this is the perfect way to use up leftover poached pears.

UPSIDE DOWN PEAR + ALMOND CAKES

SERVES **4**
30 MINUTES TO MAKE
35 MINUTES TO COOK

175G UNSALTED BUTTER, SOFTENED,
    PLUS EXTRA TO GREASE
100ML LEFTOVER SYRUP FROM STAR
    ANISE + HONEY POACHED PEARS
    (PAGE 185)
250G CASTER SUGAR
2 FREE-RANGE EGGS
125G SELF-RAISING FLOUR
50G GROUND ALMONDS
2 STAR ANISE + HONEY POACHED
    PEARS (PAGE 185)

1. Preheat the oven to 160°C/fan 140°C/gas 3 and grease 6 x 250ml ramekins.

2. Put the leftover syrup and 100g of the caster sugar in a saucepan and set over a low heat to melt the sugar. Increase the heat and boil until you have a golden amber caramel.

3. Meanwhile, beat the butter and remaining sugar together with a hand whisk until light and fluffy. Add the eggs one at a time, beating between each addition then fold in the flour and almonds.

4. Slice the pears into little wedges and put into the bottom of the ramekins. Pour the caramel over the pears evenly. Spoon the mixture on top then bake for 40–45 minutes until the sponge is risen and golden and firm to the touch. Run a knife around the edge of the ramekins, leave to stand for 2 minutes then turn out. Leave to cool a little more then serve warm.

tip If you haven't poached the pears (page 185), take 2 pears and peel and slice into wedges. Put into a pan with 150ml water and 30g caster sugar and simmer gently for about 10 minutes until just tender. Cool before using.

Using a mix of honey and almonds along with the more usual breadcrumbs and syrup makes this tart less tooth-achingly sweet than a simple treacle tart but no less moreish.

STICKY ALMOND + HONEY TART

SERVES **4**, PLUS LEFTOVERS
30 MINUTES TO MAKE
1 HOUR **20** MINUTES TO COOK

FOR THE PASTRY
200G PLAIN FLOUR, PLUS EXTRA
  TO DUST
PINCH OF SALT
110G COLD UNSALTED BUTTER, CUT
  INTO CUBES

FOR THE FILLING
100G SOFT WHITE BREADCRUMBS
80G GROUND ALMONDS
500G GOLDEN SYRUP
250G RUNNY HONEY
GRATED ZEST OF 1 LEMON
2 FREE-RANGE EGGS, BEATEN
3 TABLESPOONS DOUBLE CREAM
DOUBLE CREAM OR ICE CREAM,
  TO SERVE

1. To make the pastry, put the flour and salt in a bowl, add the butter and rub together with your fingers until it resembles breadcrumbs. Add enough water to just start to bring the mixture together with the blade of a knife.

2. Bring the pastry together with your hands and knead briefly until smooth. Roll out on a lightly floured surface and line a 23 x 3cm deep, fluted tart tin. Prick with a fork and chill for 30 minutes.

3. Preheat the oven to 200°C/fan 180°C/gas 6 and put a baking sheet in to heat up. Line the pastry case with baking parchment and baking beans or rice. Bake for 15 minutes then remove the paper and baking beans or rice and return to the oven for 5 minutes until lightly golden. Set aside and reduce the temperature to 160°C/fan 140°C/gas 3.

4. Put the breadcrumbs and almonds in a bowl. In a pan, melt the syrup and honey until it is runny then add the lemon zest. Mix well then add the eggs and cream. Pour this mixture over the breadcrumbs and almonds and leave to stand for 5 minutes until it starts to swell and absorb the liquid.

5. Pour into the pastry case and bake for 45–50 minutes until golden brown and set. Cool in the tin for 10-15 minutes then transfer to a plate and serve with cream or ice cream.

ENOUGH LEFT OVER FOR:
SEMIFREDDO SLICE (PAGE 192)
STUFFED BAKED APPLES (PAGE 194) »——→

The ultimate lazy way to make ice cream – no churning, just a little whisk and a good freeze.

SERVES **4**

25 MINUTES TO MAKE,
   PLUS FREEZING

3 LARGE FREE-RANGE EGGS, SEPARATED
90G CASTER SUGAR
400ML DOUBLE CREAM, MASCARPONE
   OR A MIXTURE
250G LEFTOVER STICKY ALMOND +
   HONEY TART (PAGE 191)

SEMIFREDDO SLICE

1. Line a 900g loaf tin (or any other similar-sized tin) with clingfilm, leaving some hanging over the edge.

2. Whisk the egg yolks with the sugar until really light and fluffy and voluminous. Add the cream or mascarpone or mixture and beat until billowy.

3. Whisk the egg whites in a clean bowl until holding stiff peaks then gently fold into the egg yolk mixture.

4. Break the leftover tart into small chunks and fold these through the mixture, being careful not to knock out any air. Carefully pour into the lined tin, covering with the excess clingfilm. Freeze for at least 12 hours.

5. About 30 minutes before you want to serve, remove from the freezer. Slice with a hot knife and serve.

tip You could be really naughty and use a bought treacle tart for this recipe or crumble up shortbread biscuits and coat them in honey and stir them into the semifreddo if you don't have any leftovers to use up.

Sometimes the most simple desserts are the best, and soft, yielding baked apples are pretty hard to beat. But they are even better with a sticky almond and honey tart centre.

SERVES **6**
15 MINUTES TO MAKE
40 MINUTES TO COOK

150-200G LEFTOVER STICKY ALMOND +
    HONEY TART (PAGE 191)
50G UNSALTED BUTTER, SOFTENED
PINCH OF GROUND ALLSPICE
GRATING OF NUTMEG
6 APPLES, SUCH AS AMBROSIA, COX
    OR OTHER EATING APPLES
CREAM, CRÈME FRAÎCHE,
    MASCARPONE OR ICE CREAM,
    TO SERVE

STUFFED BAKED APPLES

1. Preheat the oven to 180°C/fan 160°C/gas 4. Break the leftover tart up with a fork. Mix with the butter and the spices.

2. Core the apples and make a thin score around their middles. Stuff them with the honey tart mixture then stand in a baking tray. Bake for 30–40 minutes until the apples are tender. Serve with cream, crème fraîche, mascarpone or ice cream.

tip Without any leftover tart you can fill your apples with a mix of shortbread and oats. Melt a knob of butter in a pan, add 150g oats that have been lightly toasted in a low oven and 2 tablespoons of golden syrup or honey and simmer together gently. Crumble in a shortbread biscuit before using to stuff the apples.

One of my favourite London bakeries is Fabrique – a Nordic bakery which makes wonderful cinnamon and cardamom buns. This recipe is my homage to their wonderful pastries.

CARDAMOM + CINNAMON BUNS

MAKES ABOUT **18**
1 HOUR TO MAKE, PLUS RISING
15–20 MINUTES TO COOK

500ML WHOLE MILK
125G BUTTER, CUT INTO PIECES
800G STRONG WHITE BREAD FLOUR, PLUS EXTRA TO DUST
1 TEASPOON SALT
7G SACHET FAST ACTION YEAST
90G CASTER SUGAR
1 FREE-RANGE EGG

FOR THE FILLING
75G UNSALTED BUTTER, SOFTENED
1 TABLESPOON GROUND CINNAMON
½ TABLESPOON GROUND CARDAMOM
75G CASTER SUGAR

FOR THE SUGAR SYRUP
100G CASTER SUGAR
100ML WATER

1. Heat the milk with the butter in a saucepan until the butter has melted. Set aside until it is just lukewarm.

2. Tip the flour and salt into a bowl. Mix the yeast and sugar in a separate bowl with a couple of tablespoons of warm water and leave to stand for 10 minutes until frothy.

3. Add the milk, butter and yeast to the flour and mix together until you have a soft, slightly sticky dough. Tip out onto a lightly floured surface and knead for 10 minutes. Return to a clean bowl, cover with oiled clingfilm and leave in a warm place until doubled in size.

4. Beat the butter, spices and sugar together until spreadable.

5. Turn the dough out and punch down with your fingertips then roll into a rectangle about 30 x 40cm on a piece of baking parchment or a clean tea towel. Spread with the butter then roll up along the long side, using the paper or tea towel to help you. Slice into 2cm thick slices.

6. Place the buns, cut-side up, on a lightly oiled baking sheet. Cover with oiled clingfilm and set aside for 30 minutes until doubled in size. Preheat the oven to 220°C/fan 200°C/gas 7. Mix the egg with a little water and glaze the buns all over then bake for 15–20 minutes until golden and risen. Bubble the sugar and 100ml water together to form a light sugar syrup. Brush over the warm buns and leave to cool before serving.

ENOUGH LEFT OVER FOR:
CARDAMOM BUN + CREAM PUDDING (PAGE 198)
PAIN PERDU (PAGE 199) »⟶

A soft, silky pillow of a pudding, this is so much more than an average bread and butter pudding.

SERVES **4**

10 MINUTES TO MAKE,
  PLUS SOAKING

30 MINUTES TO COOK

400ML WHOLE MILK OR A MIX OF MILK
  AND CREAM
2 FREE-RANGE EGG YOLKS
1 TABLESPOON CASTER SUGAR, PLUS
  EXTRA TO SPRINKLE
BUTTER, TO GREASE
4 LEFTOVER CARDAMOM + CINNAMON
  BUNS (PAGE 195)

CARDAMOM BUN + CREAM PUDDING

1. Preheat the oven to 180°C/fan 160°C/gas 4.

2. Heat the milk (or milk and cream) in a saucepan until just boiling. Remove from the heat and set aside.

3. Beat the egg yolks and sugar in a heatproof bowl then pour the hot milk over the top and stir well. Grease a 1.2-litre ovenproof dish with butter.

4. Tear the leftover buns into pieces and arrange them in the dish then pour over the custard. Leave to soak for 15–20 minutes.

5. Bake for 25–30 minutes until softly set and golden. Scatter with caster sugar and serve.

tip If you haven't make the Cardamom + Cinnamon Buns (page 195), you could use slices of brioche or croissant instead and add a little ground cardamom and cinnamon to the custard.

This recipe is a wonderful way to turn a few day-old buns into a delicious breakfast.

SERVES **4**

15 MINUTES TO MAKE

10 MINUTES TO COOK

3 FREE-RANGE EGGS

175ML MILK

50G UNSALTED BUTTER

3-4 LEFTOVER CARDAMOM +
   CINNAMON BUNS (PAGE 195), HALVED

MAPLE SYRUP OR HONEY AND CREAM,
   CRÈME FRAÎCHE OR MASCARPONE,
   TO SERVE

PAIN PERDU

1. Whisk the eggs and the milk together in a bowl. Melt half the butter in a saucepan. Dip half the leftover buns in the eggy mixture and fry for 2 minutes on each side until set. Wipe the pan with kitchen paper and repeat with the remaining butter and buns.

2. Serve with maple syrup or honey and dollops of cream, crème fraîche or mascarpone.

tip Use slices of brioche instead of the Cardamom + Cinnamon Buns (page 195) and add a pinch of ground cardamom and cinnamon to the egg mixture.

The only things my granny could cook were meatloaf and a wonderful chocolate mousse. The latter always went wrong but somehow was more delicious for it. I've never managed to recreate her mousse but this is my version in her honour.

RICH CHOCOLATE MOUSSE

MAKES **8**

20 MINUTES TO MAKE, PLUS CHILLING

200G DARK CHOCOLATE, APPROX. 70 PER CENT COCOA SOLIDS, BROKEN INTO PIECES

150ML DOUBLE CREAM

3 LARGE FREE-RANGE EGGS, SEPARATED

45G CASTER SUGAR

1. Break the chocolate into small pieces and put in a large heatproof bowl. Heat the cream to almost boiling then pour over the chocolate. Stir to mix then add the egg yolks.

2. Whisk the egg whites in a clean bowl until they form soft peaks then gradually whisk in the sugar until you have a glossy light meringue.

3. Mix a quarter of the egg whites into the chocolate mixture to loosen it then very carefully fold in the rest, being careful not to knock out too much of the air. Spoon into 8 x 150ml glasses and chill for at least 2 hours.

ENOUGH LEFT OVER FOR:
MINI CHOC 'N' NUT ICE CREAMS (PAGE 202)
CHOCOLATE FRIDGE CAKE (PAGE 202) »——→

The idea for these came from my love of the retro ice cream 'the chocolate feast' – so this provides a bit of childhood nostalgia for a sunny day.

MINI CHOC 'N' NUT ICE CREAMS

MAKES **6**
10 MINUTES TO MAKE
3 HOURS TO FREEZE

200G LEFTOVER RICH CHOCOLATE
  MOUSSE (PAGE 201)
200G DARK CHOCOLATE APPROX.
  70 PER CENT COCOA SOLIDS, BROKEN
  INTO PIECES
50G TOASTED HAZELNUTS, CHOPPED

1. Use a mini ice cream scoop or a spoon dipped in hot water to scoop out balls or quenelles of leftover chocolate mousse. Put onto a small baking sheet lined with baking parchment then freeze until solid – this will take about 2½ hours.

2. Melt the chocolate in a heatproof bowl over a pan of barely simmering water then set aside.

3. Bring the frozen chocolate balls out of the freezer and stand on a wire rack over a baking sheet. Pour over the slightly cooled chocolate and very quickly scatter with the chopped hazelnuts. Return to the freezer to solidify.

Fridge cake reminds me of my best friend Cat who adores this chilled sweet treat. I once made it for her birthday in a battered old frying pan, which was the only vessel we had to hand.

CHOCOLATE FRIDGE CAKE

MAKES **18** SQUARES
5 MINUTES TO MAKE
5 MINUTES TO CHILL

200G LEFTOVER RICH CHOCOLATE
  MOUSSE (PAGE 201)
2 TABLESPOONS GOLDEN SYRUP
150G MIX OF YUMMY BITS, SUCH AS
  BROKEN BISCUITS, MARSHMALLOWS,
  DRIED FRUITS, HONEYCOMB AND
  NUTS (ANYTHING YOU LIKE!)

1. Put the chocolate mousse in a bowl, add the golden syrup then stir in the remaining ingredients. Pour into a small cake or loaf tin lined with baking parchment and chill until solid. Cut into cubes and serve.

tip If you don't have any leftovers, use shop-bought chocolate mousse or you can melt 75g chocolate with 75ml double cream to form a ganache. Leave it to cool a little then add the golden syrup and remaining ingredients and follow the method above.

INDEX

A

almonds: sprouting broccoli, sherry + almonds 113
   sticky almond + honey tart 191
   upside down pear + almond cake 189
anchovies: salsa verde 31
apples: apple + pecan crumble 181
   apple + pecan crumble tart 184
   pan-roasted pork chops with apples + onions 55
   red cabbage chutney 132
   shredded pork + apple buns 54
   stuffed baked apples 194
aubergines: aubergine + tomato mini calzone 137
   lamb karahi 28
   pasta bake with aubergine + tomatoes 136
   roast aubergine + tomatoes 135
   sort of moussaka 25
   Szechuan pork + aubergine bites 62

B

barley: beef + barley soup 42
beans: chicken + white beans 16
béarnaise sauce, beef with 38
beef: beef + barley soup 42
   beef summer rolls 48
   beef with béarnaise sauce + chips 38
   slow-cooked beef ragù 39
   smoky beef empanadas 43
   spice-crusted rump cap with Puy lentil salad 35
   sticky braised short ribs 45
   tagliata 36
   Thai beef salad 46
beetroot: baked beetroot with soured cream + herbs 121
   beetroot + feta cake 124
   beetroot pilaf 122
   goulash 52
berries: berry + lime pots 178
   berry compote 177
   berry ripple ice cream 179
bisque, prawn 99
brassica slaw, mixed pickled 134
broccoli: baked eggs with sprouting broccoli 114
   giant couscous + sprouting broccoli 116
   quick chicken, purple sprouting broccoli + sticky chilli stir-fry 22
   sprouting broccoli, sherry + almonds 113
bulgar wheat: tabbouleh salad 89
buns, cardamom + cinnamon 195
burgers: shredded pork + apple buns 54

C

cabbage: braised red cabbage 131
   mixed pickled brassica slaw 134
   red cabbage chutney 132
cakes: crumble cupcakes 182
   lemon fancies 168
   upside down pear + almond cake 189
calzone, aubergine + tomato mini 137
capers, pan-fried mackerel with 85
cardamom: cardamom + cinnamon buns 195
   cardamom bun + cream pudding 198
cauliflower: cauliflower cheese 107
   cauliflower cheese, cumin + turmeric fritters 110
   cauliflower cheese soup 108
   roast cod with harissa chickpeas + cauliflower 88
cheese: beetroot + feta cake 124
   cauliflower cheese 107
   cauliflower cheese, cumin + turmeric fritters 110
   cauliflower cheese soup 108
   potato + blue cheese croquettes 119
   potato + halloumi in spiced tomato sauce 147
   squash + Parmesan soufflé 156
   see also ricotta
chicken: chicken + white beans 16
   chicken Hainan 67
   chicken stock 19
   coconut + chilli chicken pots 69
   griddled chicken with kale, tarragon + hazelnut pesto 13
   linguine with kale pesto + crispy chicken skin 14
   quick chicken, purple sprouting broccoli + sticky chilli stir-fry 22
   roast chicken + mushroom risotto 20
   roast chicken with lemon + tarragon 19
   soul soup 68
chickpeas: roast cod with harissa chickpeas + cauliflower 88
   spiced lamb + hummus wraps 24
   spiced pork with harissa chickpeas 58
chillies: baked squash with chilli + rosemary 153
   coconut + chilli chicken pots 69
   quick chicken, purple sprouting broccoli + sticky chilli stir-fry 22
chips, beef with béarnaise sauce + 38
chives: mackerel, chive, leek + crème fraîche pots 86
chocolate: chocolate fridge cake 202
   mini choc 'n' nut ice creams 202
   rich chocolate mousse 201
chutney, red cabbage 132
cinnamon: cardamom + cinnamon buns 195
coconut + chilli chicken pots 69

THANK YOU

This book is so much more than a book on leftovers cooking. As a subject, leftovers are quite a tricky thing to write about, being in their nature something that you cannot predict you will have. The way it made most sense to me was to write a book about the way I cook. Always cooking a little bit more than I probably need, and keeping a well-stocked fridge and larder for fridge-raiding suppers, which have always been my favourite. I love no-rules cooking and this book explores how to use the bounty in your own kitchen to come up with some truly fun and different uses for leftovers.

I couldn't possibly have done this book on my own and there are so many wonderful people who have played a part in how beautiful and simple it is.

Firstly to my Moomin Mama – who taught me that everything is worth saving, from a single sausage to a small bowl of rice or a spoonful of sauce. Nothing is wasted in her kitchen and her love and passion for food has infiltrated my very soul.

To my dream-team girlies: Ted and her beautiful pictures, her talent for making everything look a million dollars is staggering, and my Noobs, the best sister and partner in crime, who knows me and my recipes inside out and always knows how best to make them shine in her wonderful props and scenes. Without you ladies this book would never be as perfect. Thank you, as always, from the bottom of my heart.

To my gorge assistants, Katie and April. The biggest thanks and hugs to you both for your amazing kitchen skills and for keeping things shipshape and running smoothly. I truly would be lost without you!

Huge thanks to Vicky, my editor, and the wonderful Kyle for allowing me to write such a dreamy book and turn the subject of leftovers into one of excitement and beauty. Thank you for putting up with me and producing such a wonderful book.

Thank you to all my family and friends for your endless tasting and re-tasting of dishes, and for all your support and love.